Herman Hertzberger

Herman van Bergeijk

Birkhäuser Verlag
Basel · Boston · Berlin

Translation English/German:
Ute Spengler, Amden

A CIP catalogue record for this book is available from the
Library of Congress, Washington D.C., USA

Deutsche Bibliothek – Cataloging-in-Publication Data

Hertzberger, Herman:
Herman Hertzberger / Herman van Bergeijk.
[Transl. Engl.-German: Ute Spengler, Amden]. - Basel ; Boston ; Berlin :
Birkhäuser, 1997
  (Studiopaperback)
  ISBN 3-7643-5698-7 (Basel …)
  ISBN 0-8176-5698-7 (Boston)

© 1997 Birkhäuser – Verlag für Architektur, P.O. Box 133,
CH-4010 Basel, Switzerland
Printed on acid-free paper produced from chlorine-free pulp. TCF ∞
Layout/page layout: Christoph Kloetzli, Basel
Printed in Germany

ISBN 3-7643-5698-7
ISBN 0-8176-5698-7

9 8 7 6 5 4 3 2 1

Inhalt

Contents

Das Werk von Herman Hertzberger

The Work of Herman Hertzberger

Die Welt von heute ist einem raschen Wandel unterworfen, der nicht ihr Wesen, so doch ihr Erscheinungsbild betrifft. Aus einem Ort der Gastlichkeit wird immer mehr ein Ort der Ausbeutung, ein Verbrauchsgut in jedem Sinn. Dieser Prozeß läßt auch die Architektur nicht unberührt, die in den Malstrom des Wandels hineingezogen worden ist und sich zur Zeit, vielleicht mehr noch als die übrigen Künste, mit dem Phänomen des Neuen als Tradition konfrontiert sieht: Sie muß neuartige, ins Auge fallende Bilder schaffen, die nicht immer die Gegenwart reflektieren, sondern häufig die Stufe eines unbestimmten Werdens vorwegnehmen oder eine oberflächliche Nostalgie artikulieren. Es ist schwer, sich diesem Modetrend zu entziehen – zu stark ist die Furcht, als unzeitgemäß abgeschrieben zu werden. Will man auf einem internationalen Markt mithalten, der zunehmend imageabhängig wird, so ist man gezwungen, mit der Zeit zu gehen. Wer an eine Architektur glaubt, die nicht nur als Bedeutungsträger und Exponent einer visuellen Kultur, sondern auch als Katalysator sozialer Beziehungen fungiert, wird das nur widerwillig akzeptieren.

Der niederländische Architekt Herman Hertzberger gehört zu denen, die nicht bereit sind, sich zu verstecken – weder hinter der Autonomie des Faches noch hinter der neurotischen Attitüde, eine bloße Kultur der Bilder zu bedienen. Mehr als jeder andere Architekt seiner Generation hat sich Hertzberger drei Themen verschrieben, die seine Arbeit von Anfang an bestimmten: den Themen Form, Funktion und Freiheit. Keines dieser Sujets ist jemals im eigentlichen Sinne beherrschend geworden. Der Spielraum, den das dritte schuf, ließ ihm immer die Möglichkeit, eigenen Ideen – nicht nur über das Bauen, sondern auch über die Gesellschaft im allgemeinen – Ausdruck zu geben. Hertzberger ist in den Niederlanden der führende Vertreter der Generation junger Nachkriegsarchitekten, einer Generation, die aus dem Ungewissen heraus an der Praxis und dogmatischen Gewißheit der niederländischen Nachkriegsarchitektur scharfe Kritik übte.

Unzufrieden mit den Ergebnissen des schnellen Wieder-

The world is changing rapidly, if not in substance, then at least in appearance. Instead of a hospitable place, it has become an increasingly exploitable one, consumable in every possible way.

This has not been without effect on architecture, which has been pulled into in the maelstrom. Perhaps even more than the other arts, it is dealing with the issue of the tradition of the new. It has to produce new eye catching images, which do not always reflect the state of being, but either anticipate the phase of undefined becoming or illustrate a superficial nostalgia. Contemporary fashion is hard to resist, as the fear of being labeled obsolete is all too present. One has to be on the wave in order to compete on the international market which is rapidly becoming merely image-dependent. Believing that architecture is not only a mediator of meaning and an exponent of a visual culture, but also a catalyser of social interactions, this is hard to accept. The Dutch architect Herman Hertzberger is one of those who do not want to hide behind the autonomy of the discipline or behind a neurotic attitude of contributing to a purely visual culture.

More than any other architect of his generation, Hertzberger dealt with three issues which have determined his architecture since the beginning: form, function and freedom. None of the three has ever prevailed in a strict sense. On the contrary, the margins which the last one created have always provided him the room to give expression to his own ideas, not only about architecture, but also about society in general. Hertzberger has been the most dominant figure of a generation of young post-war architects; a generation of uncertainty which severely criticized the praxis and dogmatism of post-war architecture in the Netherlands. Not convinced by the results of the rapid post-war reconstruction, they pleaded for an orientation in a totally different direction. The heroic tradition of modern architecture could no longer provide the necessary solutions, but a rethinking about architecture and its meanings in a democratic society had to form the basis for a fresh start with man at its center. Partly, one had

aufbaus, plädierte man für eine radikale Neuorientierung. Die notwendigen Lösungen wurden nicht mehr in der heroischen Tradition des modernen Bauens gesucht: Ein neues Verständnis der Architektur und ihrer Bedeutung in einer demokratischen Gesellschaft sollte die Grundlage für einen Neubeginn bilden, in dessen Zentrum der Mensch stand. Dazu gehörte das Studium einer «kleinen Anzahl einzigartiger Bauwerke, die den Mechanismus der Architektur des zwanzigsten Jahrhunderts repräsentieren.» Diese neue Sehweise stand für eine ungeteilte Einheit aller Lebensbereiche. Die Architektur sollte kein Sonderdasein führen, vielmehr wie die Kunst als elementares Bedürfnis des Menschen gelten. Ihre geistigen Führer fanden die jungen Architekten dieser Generation – Hertzberger, Joop van Stigt, Piet Blom, D.C. Apon u. a. – in Aldo van Eyck und Jaap Bakema. Sie waren innerhalb der Gruppe «Team X» hervorgetreten und vertraten in den heftig geführten Auseinandersetzungen jener Zeit verwandte und doch voneinander abweichende Positionen. Die flammenden Vorträge und Artikel van Eycks eröffneten ebenso wie sein berühmtes Amsterdamer Waisenhaus einen Horizont, der für viele Architekten und ihre Vorstellungen wegweisend wurde. Bakema trat bei den Debatten als Konkurrent und Mitstreiter van Eycks auf; er brachte aber vor allem durch sein architektonisches Werk neue Perspektiven und Ausgangspunkte ins Spiel.

Hertzberger wurde mit beiden gut bekannt, nachdem er sich 1959 auf Anfrage dem neu gebildeten Redaktionsteam der Zeitschrift «Forum» angeschlossen hatte, die bis dahin offizielles Sprachrohr der Architektenvereinigung Architectura und Amicitia gewesen war. In diesem Jahr hatte das alte Redaktionskolleg eine Nummer der Zeitschrift einem ungewöhnlichen Thema gewidmet: der Kunst der «Liga nieuwe beelden», auf den hin van Eyck mit dem Manifest «Die Geschichte einer anderen Idee» replizierte und so eine neue Artikelserie auslöste. Seine Ideen und Vorstellungen wurden in den folgenden Nummern aufgegriffen und vertieft, so in dem Heft über «Die Form des Dazwischen». Dort zeigte Hertzberger, wie sich in Wohnhausprojekten Schwellenzonen verwirklichen lassen, und veranschaulichte seine Vorschläge mit Modellen aus Streichholzschachteln. So wurde «Forum» für Hertzberger zu einer zweiten Ausbildungsstätte, in der er sich mit Themen vertraut machte, die sein künftiges Bauen maßgeblich bestimmten. Er begann bewußt darauf zu achten, wie Menschen zueinander in Beziehung stehen und inwieweit die gebaute Umgebung zur Intensivierung von Kommunikation beiträgt. Soziale Themen haben Hertzberger seit seinen beruflichen Anfängen beschäftigt; er war ein produktiver Autor und wirkte als anregender Lehrer an zahlreichen Hochschulen. Vor allem aber war

to study a "small collection of unique buildings representing the mechanism of 20th century architecture." This new view propagated the undivided unity of all sectors of life. Architecture should be viewed as a basic need of man. A generation of young architects, like Hertzberger, Joop van Stigt, Piet Blom, and D.C. Apon, found their inspirational leaders in the figures of Aldo van Eyck and Jaap Bakema. The latter two had established their position within the group of Team X and represented similar yet different poles in the heated discussions of those days. The flaming talks and articles of Van Eyck, as well as his famous Orphanage in Amsterdam, opened up a horizon which was to be crucial to many architects. Bakema, on the other hand, rivaled Van Eyck in the discussions, but it was, above all, in his architectural work that he initiated new views and points of departure. Hertzberger became well acquainted with them after he had been asked to join the new editorial board of the magazine Forum in 1959 which, until that moment, had been the official mouthpiece of the architecture association "Architectura et Amicitia". In that year, after the old editorial staff had dedicated the last issue of the magazine to an unusual subject, the art of the "Liga nieuwe beelden", Van Eyck launched a new cycle with the manifesto "the story of another idea". His ideas and concepts were taken up and elaborated in subsequent issues, like the one dedicated to "the Form of the In-between" in which Hertzberger

Santa Maria del Fiore, Florence, 1959

und ist er Architekt und Baumeister: In seinen Bauten verwirklicht er seine Ideen.

Kurz vor Erscheinen der ersten Nummer des erneuerten «Forum» hatte Hertzberger bei M. Duintjer sein Studium am Delfter Polytechnikum abgeschlossen. Duintjer hatte für Le Corbusier gearbeitet, und einzelne seiner Bauwerke zeichnen sich durch einen gemäßigten, doch formvollendeten Funktionalismus aus. Bereits während seiner Ausbildung hatte Hertzberger an mehreren Wettbewerben teilgenommen und in seinem letzten Studienjahr zusammen mit T. Hazewinkel ein Wettbewerbsprojekt für ein Studentenheim in Amsterdam entworfen, das mit dem ersten Preis ausgezeichnet wurde. Obwohl Hazewinkel nach dem Studium zum Militärdienst eingezogen wurde und das Projekt in veränderter Form erst einige Jahre später zur Ausführung gelangte, gab dieser gewichtige Erfolg dem jungen Architekten den Anstoß, ein eigenes Büro zu eröffnen. Das Studentenheim zeigt Hertzbergers lebenslange Faszination durch das Werk Le Corbusiers, «dessen Interesse niemals der Form galt, sondern immer dem «Funktionsmechanismus». Das Gebäude zeigt in Ideen und Konzepten eine deutliche Verwandtschaft mit den Unités d'habitation. Das Thema der oberen «Wohnstraße», die eine Verbindung zu den Dächern der Nachbargebäude schafft, läßt sich indessen bis zum Spangen-Komplex von Michiel Brinkman in Rotterdam zurückverfolgen. Dieses Gestaltungsdetail sowie seine Artikulierung und intelligente Eingliederung sind nicht nur Ausdruck eines sorgfältig durchdachten Entwurfs, sie setzen das Gebäude auch auf besondere Weise in Beziehung zu seiner Umgebung: Als Ganzes bildet der Bau einen Übergang von den höheren Gebäuden der belebten Weesperstraat zu den niedrigeren Häusern an den Grachten.

Die ersten Aufträge des neuen Büros Hertzberger waren die Montessorischule in Delft (1960–1966) und die Erweiterung der Wäscherei LinMij in Amsterdam (1962–1964). Beide Projekte wurden in mehreren Architekturzeitschriften publiziert und trugen zur wachsenden Bekanntheit des jungen Architekten bei. Die zwei jüngeren Gebäude lassen gegenüber dem Studentenheim ein leicht verändertes Interesse erkennen. Stimuliert durch die abendlichen Sitzungen der «Forum»-Redaktion und unter dem Eindruck der in seinem Umkreis stattfindenden sozialen und künstlerischen Entwicklungen wie der Gruppe Nul, ging Hertzberger daran, neue Möglichkeiten zu erproben. Die Nähwerkstatt der Wäscherei war ein Erweiterungsbau auf dem Dach des alten Gebäudes. Der neue Baukörper aus Beton-Fertigstützen und Trägerbalken aus Stahlbeton nutzte den Altbau als Sockel und sollte diesen in Zukunft überwuchern, wenn weitere Anbauten nötig würden. Das bestehende Gebäude und seine Erweiterung

demonstrated how threshold areas can be introduced in housing projects, illustrating his article with models made of match boxes. Forum was for Hertzberger a second training school, where he became acquainted with themes which would be central to his future architecture. He developed an attention to the way people interacted and to the extent which the built environment contributed to an intensification of communication. Since the beginning of his career, Hertzberger has been a social thinker, a prolific writer and an inspiring lecturer who has taught in many universities. Above all, he is an architect. Through his buildings, he verifies his ideas.

Shortly before the first new issue of Forum came out, Hertzberger finished his studies at the Polytechnical University at Delft where he graduated under professor M. Duintjer who had worked for Le Corbusier and whose architecture sometimes expressed a weak but refined functionalism. During his architectural education, Hertzberger participated in several competitions, and in the last year at the University he entered, together with T. Hazewinkel, the winning project in a competition for a student hostel in Amsterdam. Although Hazewinkel was drafted after his studies and the modified project would be executed a few years later, this significant success provided a reason for the opening of his own office. The student hostel (1959–1966) shows Hertzberger's lifelong fascination with the work of Le Corbusier, "who was never occupied with form, but always with the mechanism he had in front of him." The building clearly expresses ideas and concepts close to those of the Unité d'habitation, although the upper "living street" between the roofs of the adjacent buildings is an idea that can be traced back to the Spangen Complex of Michiel Brinkman in Rotterdam. Through this feature, as well as its articulation and its intelligent juxtaposition, the building is not only a carefully designed object, but also relates in an interesting way to the surrounding environment. The building in itself forms a transition from the higher buildings on the busy Weesperstraat to the lower ones on the canals. The first commissions for the studio Hertzberger were the Montessori School in Delft (1960–1966) and the extension to the LinMij Laundry in Amsterdam (1962–1964). Both projects were published in several architectural magazines and contributed to the fame of the young architect. These two buildings show slightly different interests than the student hostel. Stimulated by the night meetings of the board of Forum and with a keen eye on social and artistic developments around him, such as those of the "Nul" group, Hertzberger started investigating other avenues. The sewing workshop of the LinMij was an extension on top of the old building. The new structure of pre-

waren im Charakter völlig verschieden. Gegen die düstere Nüchternheit des alten Ziegelbaus setzte der Anbau Leichtigkeit und Licht. Er brachte die Poesie verletzlicher Nacktheit zum Ausdruck; «Altes und Neues verleihen einander Identität», erklärte der Architekt. Die Suche nach Identität war eines der Hauptthemen der «Forum»-Gruppe, und man sah sich auch in älteren Kulturen nach Lösungen um. 1962 war eine Ausgabe von «Forum» den Pueblos gewidmet. Es ist deshalb sicher kein Zufall, daß dieser Anbau mehr oder weniger wie ein Pueblo auf den farblosen, massiven Altbau gesetzt ist.

Einige Jahre später beschäftigte sich Hertzberger in einem Artikel mit dem Problem der Identität und stellte fest: «Wir müssen die Möglichkeit für individuelle Deutungen schaffen, das heißt die Dinge so gestalten, daß sie tatsächlich deutbar werden. (...) Wir deuten die Form, aber die Form deutet auch uns, zeigt uns etwas von dem, was wir sind. So beginnen Form und Benutzer sich wechselseitig zu interpretieren. Sie stärken einander in ihrer Individualität, und prägen somit beide ihre Eigenart aus.» Im Entwurf für die Montessorischule in Delft war der Gedanke der Identität bei der Raumgestaltung von entscheidender Bedeutung. Es wurden zahlreiche Zonen geschaffen, die den Kindern Gelegenheit geben, ihre Phantasie zu entwickeln und sich den Raum anzueignen. Der Eingang der Schule ist nicht einfach durch die Türe festgelegt, sondern besteht aus einem Übergangsbereich, der beiden Räumen, sowohl der Schule wie der Außenwelt, angehört. Die Schwelle ist eliminiert. Der Flur ist kein simpler Durchgang, sondern ein Raum, der sich auf verschiedene Art nutzen läßt – er ist zu einer weiten Halle geworden. In seinen erläuternden Anmerkungen zum Projekt erwähnt der Architekt, er habe im Hinblick auf zukünftige Erweiterungen ein Ordnungssystem geschaffen, innerhalb dessen jeder Anbau eine abgeschlossene Einheit bilden könne und dennoch zur Vervollständigung des Ganzen beitrage. Bausteine dieser Ordnung wurden die L-förmigen Klassenräume, die sich mit dem nachdrücklich artikulierten Vestibül verbinden ließen. Ein augenfälliges Element an der Außenseite sind die kubischen Oberlichter, durch die das Vestibül belichtet wird und die dem relativ niedrigen Gebäude zusammen mit den hohen Klassenzimmern eine lebendige Silhouette verleihen.

Dasselbe Prinzip – die Artikulation des Gebäudes durch die Anordnung der verschiedenen Volumen zu einer Art Stufenturm, – ist im Wettbewerbsbeitrag für eine Kirche in Driebergen (1964) als Abfolge von Dachterrassen, als Dachlandschaft, realisiert. Außer Hertzberger waren fünf weitere junge Architekten zu diesem Wettbewerb geladen. Die Aufgabe lautete, in Zusammenarbeit mit einem Künstler einen Entwurf vorzulegen, aus dem ein Gottes-

fabricated supports and beams of reinforced concrete used the old building as a foundation, and was meant to overgrow it slowly in the future, when further extensions would be necessary. The existing building and the extension differed greatly in character. The old brick building was sober and dark; the extension brought lightness and light. The extension expressed the poetry of a vulnerable nudity. As the architect said: "old and new provide each other identity."

The search for identity was a main theme for the members of the Forum group. They looked at older cultures for solutions. One of the issues of Forum in 1962 was dedicated to the Pueblos. It can not be a coincidence that the extension is situated like a pueblo on top of the old colorless and massive building. Some years later, Hertzberger would dedicate an article to the problem of identity. He stated: "... we have to create the possibility for personal interpretation by making things in such a way that they are indeed interpretable. ... Not only do we interpret the form, the form simultaneously interprets us; it shows us something of who we are. Thus, user and form begin mutually to interpret each other; their identities are strengthened by each other; each becomes more itself." In the design of the Montessori School in Delft, the role of identity in relation to place is of crucial importance. There are many zones where the children can develop their fantasies and appropriate the space. The entrance to the school is not simply defined by the door, but consists of a transitional area which belongs to both the school and the outside world. The threshold is eliminated. The corridor is not a simple passage, but a space which can be used in various ways. It becomes a large hall. In his explanatory note of the project the architect mentions that, due to the fact that the building would be extended in the future, he created a building order that would permit every extension to be complete in itself as well as to complete the whole. The single L-formed classrooms became the building blocks which could be linked to the highly articulated hall. A striking element on the outside is the cubic skylights that give light to the hall and which, together with the high classrooms, give a lively silhouette to this relatively low building.

The same principle of giving articulation to the building by a zigzag-like placing of the volumes which then form a number of roof terraces, a roof landscape, can be found in his competition entry for a church in Driebergen (1964). Hertzberger and five other young architects were invited to make a design in collaboration with an artist which would lead to a new type of church, a meeting-place of sorts. Hertzberger refused to work with an artist. He made "an architectonic space with a diaphragmatic character in

haus neuer Art, ein Ort der Begegnung, hervorgehen sollte. Hertzberger lehnte es ab, mit einem Künstler zusam-
menzuarbeiten. Er schuf «einen spiralförmig angelegten
architektonischen Raum mit halbdurchlässigem Charakter». Die Jurymitglieder, unter ihnen Bakema und Gerrit
Rietveld, bewunderten die bauliche Qualität und plasti-
sche Intensität von Hertzbergers Projekt; sie vermißten jedoch Leichtigkeit und Ruhe und sprachen den ersten Preis
dem Beitrag Aldo van Eycks zu.

Kurz darauf entstand Hertzbergers erster Entwurf eines
Wohnheims für Betagte, «De Drie Hoven» (1964–1974),
das einen durchgehenden räumlichen Raster auf der
Basis eines einzigen Modulelements vorsah. Diese Kon-
struktion ermöglichte es ihm, den Anforderungen des
äußerst vielfältigen und hochkomplexen Programms auf
flexible Weise gerecht zu werden. Gleichzeitig erlaubte
es, «Orte» für zufällige Begegnungen zu schaffen, die
den Bewohnern das Gefühl der Zugehörigkeit zur Welt
vermitteln sollten.

Ein bedeutendes Projekt im Gesamtwerk Hertzbergers ist
zweifellos der Wettbewerbsbeitrag für das Rathaus von
Valkenswaard (1966). In diesem Projekt mit dem Namen
«Het Glazen Slot» (Das gläserne Schloß) setzte der Architekt die Arbeit am Thema der strukturellen Konfiguration
fort, das mit van Eycks Amsterdamer Waisenhaus Eingang
in die niederländische Architektur gefunden hatte. Nach
Ansicht van Eycks sollte eine Stadt «eine Hierarchie sich
überlagernder, multilateral konzipierter struktureller Systeme bilden. (…) Alle Systeme sollten so miteinander
verwandt sein, daß ihre gesammelte Wirkung und Wech-
selwirkung als ein einziges komplexes System wahrzu-
nehmen ist – polyphonisch, von rhythmischer Vielfalt, ka-
leidoskopisch und dennoch in jedem Moment und allent-
halben verständlich: eine einheitliche, homogene
Konfiguration aus zahlreichen Subsystemen, die sich auf
ein Generalthema beziehen und in ihm legitimiert sind,
sich jedoch in der Binnenstruktur, im Grad der Bewegung
sowie im Assoziationspotential unterscheiden.» Hertzbergers häufig betonte Wertschätzung van Eycks sollte
indes nicht zu einer allzu einfachen, linearen Deutung ver-
leiten. Die Arbeitsweise der zwei Architekten läßt deutliche Unterschiede erkennen. Entschiedener als van Eyck,
der sich zu oft von der Poesie seiner programmatischen
Erklärungen faszinieren ließ, ging Hertzberger daran, das
architektonische Potential seiner Ideen auszuloten. Im
Gegensatz zu van Eyck sah Hertzberger die Sprache der
Architektur als ein Problem, das intensive systematische
Untersuchung und Bearbeitung verlangte und sich nicht
auf Poesie reduzieren ließ, wenn sie den Sinn für Identität
stärken sollte. In Analogie zur Linguistik wurde die Kultur
bedeutsame Beziehung zwischen «langue» und «paro-

St. Ivo della Sapienza, Rome, 1959

the form of a spiral". The jury, of which Bakema and Gerrit
Rietveld were part, admired the architectural quality and
plastic intensity of Hertzberger's project, but sensed a lack
of easing in the tension. The first prize was awarded to the
entry of Aldo van Eyck.

Shortly thereafter, Hertzberger made the first design of
the residential building for elderly people "De Drie
Hoven" (1964–1974) which would lead to the use of a
single continuous structural framework based on one
modular unit. This framework permitted him to deal in a
flexible way with the requirements of the highly varied
and complex program. At the same time, it made it possible to create "places" where the people could encounter
each other and get a feeling of belonging to the world.

An important project, certainly within the complete oeuvre of Hertzberger, is the competition entry for the Town
Hall of Valkenswaard (1966). In this project with the
motto "Het Glazen Slot" (the glass castle), the architect
continued his research of the theme of configuration, initiated in the Netherlands by Van Eyck in his Orphanage in
Amsterdam. In the opinion of Van Eyck, a city "should em-
brace a hierarchy of superimposed configurative systems
multilaterally conceived … All systems should be famil-
iarized, one with the other, in such a way that their combined impact and interaction can be appreciated as a
single complex system – polyphonal, multi-rhythmic,
kaleidoscopic and yet perpetually and everywhere com-
prehensible: a single homogeneous configuration com-

le», zwischen dem Sprachsystem und den einzelnen menschlichen Sprechakten, und ihre Entsprechung in der Tektonik der Architektur zum vorherrschenden Thema seines Werks. Ohne den künstlerischen Wert aus dem Blick zu verlieren, verfolgte er sein Interesse an den strukturalen und systematischen Seiten der Architektur. Er ging dabei aber nie so weit wie N. J. Habraken, der die anthropologische Dimension des Bauens unberücksichtigt ließ. Für Hertzberger bestand die gesellschaftliche Funktion der Architektur nicht allein darin, primäre menschliche Bedürfnisse zu erfüllen. Er sah in ihr den Raum, in dem die Mitglieder der Gesellschaft einander begegnen, und maß ihr eine über das Pragmatische hinausgehende, in erster Linie kreative und aktive Bedeutung zu. Seine Bauten verstand er nicht nur als Bilder einer Gesellschaft im Wandel, sondern auch als Subjekt dieses Wandels, als Geburtshelfer der neuen Gesellschaft.

In seinem Konzept für das Rathaus von Valkenswaard ging Hertzberger von dem Gedanken aus, daß Publikum und Stadtverwaltung in ständigem wechselseitigen Kontakt stehen. Diesen demokratischen Grundsatz sollte der Entwurf repräsentieren, eine Vorstellung, die der Architekt auch in seinem Vergleich des Gebäudes mit einem Kaufhaus ausdrückt. Er entwarf ein Gebäude aus zahlreichen einzelnen Blöcken oder Türmen in Rasteranordnung; den Raum zwischen den Blöcken konzipierte er als öffentliche Verkehrsfläche. Eine Vierergruppe, in der die wichtigsten Ratssäle untergebracht sind, bildete das Zentrum des Gebäudekomplexes. Der unhierarchische Charakter der Blockeinheiten sollte künftige Erweiterungen erleichtern. Der Architekt entwarf ein Bausystem aus Fertigelementen, die sich zu Stockwerken stapeln ließen. Die Geschoßflächen sollten frei bleiben und nach Bedarf ausgefüllt werden. Die konservative Jury würdigte die Originalität des Entwurfs, hielt die Anlage jedoch für unzweckmäßig und gab zu bedenken, daß die Besucher auf der Suche nach ihren Zielorten durch den Gebäudekomplex irren könnten. Man muß in diesem Zusammenhang daran erinnern, daß der Entwurf aus der Zeit vor 1968 stammt, in der solche emanzipatorischen Ideen noch als Bedrohung des Establishments und seiner Werte empfunden wurden. Es kann daher nicht überraschen, daß auch Hertzbergers Wettbewerbsprojekt für das Rathaus von Amsterdam (1967) – ein im wesentlichen verwandter Entwurf – bei den Juroren auf Ablehnung stieß. In seiner Darstellung des Projekts schrieb der Architekt: «Man geht nicht ins Rathaus, um eine bestimmte Dienstleistung zu verlangen, sondern um bedient zu werden. In diesem Sinne muß ein Rathaus also wesentlich anti-monumental sein. Das Gebäude versucht nicht, sich von seiner Umgebung abzusondern, sondern sich weitestgehend in den unmittelba-

Segesta, Sicily, 1960

posed of many sub-systems, each covering the same overall area and each valid, but each with a different grain, scale of movement, and association potential." The often signalized reverence of Hertzberger for Van Eyck should not lead to easy and linear interpretations. There are distinct differences in the way the two operated. More than Van Eyck, who was often fascinated by the poetic quality of his own statements, Hertzberger started elaborating the architectural potential of his ideas. In contrast to Van Eyck, the language of architecture was, for Hertzberger, much more a problem to be studied and investigated in a systematic way. It could not be reduced to mere poetry; certainly not if it wanted to contribute to a major sense of identity. In analogy to linguistics: the cultural relation between "parole" and "langue" and its representation in the tectonics of architecture became predominant in his work. Without dismissing its artistic values, Hertzberger became more and more interested in the structural and systematic qualities of architecture. This never went so far as in the work of N.J. Habraken, who had no regard for the anthropological dimension of architecture. For Hertzberger, architecture did not serve society in the sense that it only fulfilled primary needs, but it is the space where the members of society encounter each other. Its role, in addition to being pragmatic, was above all creative and active. He conceived of his buildings not only as the images of a changing society, but also as the agents which were destined to bring that society about.

In the concept for the Town Hall in Valkenswaard,

ren städtischen Kontext zu integrieren.» Offen bleibt die Frage, ob das Projekt als Versuch zu betrachten ist, ein Ordnungsprinzip zu finden, das der Stadtstruktur gerecht wird. Verglichen mit dem Projekt für Valkenswaard, war das Zentrum dieses Gebäudes in Größe, Form und Bedeutung differenzierter geplant, doch in den Randzonen läßt der Entwurf durchaus einen Bezug zur historischen Substanz dieses Teils von Amsterdam vermissen. Dagegen ist die Erschließung optimal gelöst: Das System von Wegen, die den Komplex durchschneiden, verknüpft die vier Ecken des Grundstücks und macht das Rathaus damit zum Knotenpunkt eines regelmäßigen Labyrinths. Es entbehrt nicht der Ironie, daß der für die Volksvertretung von Valkenswaard und Amsterdam vorgeschlagene Entwurf durch eine Versicherungsgesellschaft zur Ausführung kam. Hertzberger teilt damit das Schicksal von Berlage, dessen erste bedeutendere Gebäude ebenfalls im Auftrag von Versicherungen entstanden.

Das veränderte Klima von 1968 machte den Weg frei für andere Formen der Repräsentation. Das Bürogebäude Centraal Beheer in Apeldoorn (1968–1972) wurde zu einem baulichen Exempel dieser Demokratisierung und zu einem der meistdiskutierten Projekte des folgenden Jahrzehnts. Es kann zugleich als eine der wesentlichen Leistungen Hertzbergers gelten, als eine Veranschaulichung und Synthese seiner Forschungen. Es ging hierbei weniger darum, Raum für Arbeitsplätze zu schaffen, als einen Raum, der von seinen Benutzern gestaltet werden konnte und zur Kommunikation einlud. Das Raumsystem umfaßt Gruppen quadratischer Büroinseln, die durch Laufstege und von oben belichtete Lufträume getrennt sind.

Alan Colquhoun faßt das Gebäude als «Superblock» auf, als ein «selbstregulierendes Aggregat aus relativ kleinen Einheiten, bei dem die zentrale Kontrolle auf ein Minimum reduziert ist.» Er zitiert zwar Albertis Feststellung, daß ein Gebäude eine kleine Stadt, und eine Stadt ein großes Gebäude sei, sieht Hertzberger aber dennoch als einen jener «großen Vereinfacher der Moderne, für die die Architektur nichts anderes ist als die Demonstration des einen oder anderen theoretischen Prinzips». Diese Einschätzung greift indessen zu kurz. Sie übergeht die Stoßrichtung des Prinzips und die geplante Nutzung des Gebäudes, das als Ort konzipiert ist, an dem Menschen soziale Beziehungen knüpfen oder intensivieren können. Colquhoun versteht das Gebäude nur im Kontext der Moderne und vermißt darum eine Vermittlung «von innerer Vielfalt und äußerer Ruhe». Er verkennt, daß der Entwurf Hertzbergers viel eher vom Paradigma des Pueblos ausgeht, an das ja auch Albertis Bemerkung denken läßt. Darüber hinaus ist an Lewis Mumford zu erinnern, der 1940 erklärte: «Das ei-

Hertzberger was led by the thought that the public and the administrators had to visit each other on mutual ground. The building had to represent this democratic principle. The architect compared it to a department store. In the project, he conceived of a building which consisted of a large number of blocks or towers laid out according to a grid-iron system. Between the blocks was the public circulation area. The nucleus of the building was a group of four blocks which contained the main auditoriums. Due to the non-hierarchical character of the blocks, future additions could easily be made. The structure was of prefabricated elements which were stacked on top of each other in order to form the storys. The floors were free and could be filled in according to needs. The traditionalist jury recognized the originality of the design, but doubted its practical use and thought that the public would roam through the building in search of their destination. One should not forget that the design dates from the before 1968 when such ideas of freedom were still considered a menace to the establishment and its values. It is, therefore, not strange that Hertzberger's entry for the town hall competition of Amsterdam (1967), which essentially showed the same scheme, was rejected as well. In the statement accompanying his project the architect wrote: "One goes to the town hall not merely to request a particular service, but to be served. In this respect, the town hall must be essentially anti-monumental. The building does not try to stand apart from the surrounding city, but on the contrary, to fit in as much as possible into the urban environment." It is still questionable if the project could be regarded as an effort to try and find a principle of order, attuned to the city structure. The core was more differentiated in size, form and meaning than that in the project of Valkenswaard, but the periphery of the design showed an independence in regard to the historic tissue of this part of Amsterdam. The accessibility of the complex was optimal. The system of roads cutting through the building pulled together the four corners of the site, and thus the town hall became a knot imbedded in a regular maze.

Ironically enough, the scheme proposed for Valkenswaard and Amsterdam for the democratic seats of these towns was brought into reality by an insurance company. Hertzberger shared the fate of Berlage, whose first major buildings were also for insurance companies. The changed climate of 1968 brought possibilities for other ways of representation, and the office building "Centraal Beheer" in Apeldoorn (1968–1972) became an example of this democratization and one of the most discussed projects of the next decade. It can be regarded as one of Hertzberger's major achievements, illustrating and synthesizing

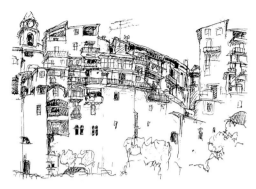

Rocchetta, Italy, 1982

gentliche Symbol der Architektur des modernen Zeitalters ist die Abwesenheit optischer Symbole: Wir suchen nicht länger an der Oberfläche, was wir nur dadurch wirksam erreichen können, daß wir in die Funktion eines Gebäudes eindringen und an ihr teilhaben.» In Anwendung der Begriffe von Lévi-Strauss ließe sich sagen, Hertzberger sucht nach dem schwierigen Gleichgewicht von Struktur und Ereignis. Eine offene Struktur wie das Raster ist kein Werkzeug der Gestaltung, keine stützende Hilfskonstruktion im Entwurfsprozeß, die am Ende entfernt wird; sie bleibt vielmehr erkennbar und sichtbar. In Übereinstimmung mit den Vorstellungen des französischen Architekten Henri Labrouste geht diese Architektur im wesentlichen aus der Struktur des Plans hervor, die Freiheit stiftet, indem sie dem Unerwarteten Raum läßt und zu einem reicheren Gemeinschaftsleben führt. Hertzberger hat nie aufgehört zu betonen, daß der Unterschied zwischen «Kompetenz» (Deutungspotential der Form) und «Performanz» (wie die Form in einer bestimmten Situation und Zeit interpretiert wird) ein zentrales Element des Strukturalismus ist. Centraal Beheer gilt als das einzige «Meisterwerk» der niederländischen Architektur der siebziger Jahre.

Gleichzeitig mit Centraal Beheer entstanden einige experimentelle Entwürfe für Wohnhäuser, von denen nur die Diagoon-Häuser in Delft realisiert wurden. Die Grundidee entspricht der des Bürogebäudes, doch an die Stelle der dichten Gruppierung und der «Landschaft aus Dachterrassen» tritt eine Verknüpfung der einzelnen Blöcke zu Ketten mit wechselnder Vorder– und Rückfront der Häuser. Die Entscheidung über die Einteilung und Nutzung der Räume bleibt den Bewohnern überlassen. Diesem Prinzip hat der Architekt noch deutlicher Ausdruck gegeben: Die Häuser sind unvollständig, und das offene Raumsystem läßt zahlreiche Möglichkeiten zur Veränderung und Umgestaltung. Laut Hertzberger ist «der Raster … eine Konstante und repräsentiert sozusagen die Ordnung, in deren Rahmen die Freiheit des einzelnen im Verhältnis zur Freiheit aller durchgespielt und in Grenzen gehalten werden

his research. The idea was not to create so much a working space, but a space which could be transformed by the users and which "invited" communication. The diagram comprises clusters of square office islands separated by walkways and toplit voids.

Alan Colquhoun sees the building as a "superblock", as "a self-regulating aggregate of relatively small parts, with any centralized control reduced to a minimum." Although he refers to Alberti's statement that a building was a small city, and a city a large building, he places Hertzberger among "those grands simplificateurs of the Modern Movement for whom architecture is simply the demonstration of some internal principle." This view is, however, too reductive and disregards both the purpose of the principle and the intended use of the building as a place where people can establish or intensify their social contacts. Colquhoun clearly reads the building purely within the context of the Modern Movement and therefore misses an integration "between internal multiplicity and external calm". He doesn't take into account how much the paradigm of the pueblo, which evokes the statement of Alberti, seems to be much more at the basis of Hertzbergers design. Besides, Lewis Mumford had concluded in 1940: "The true symbol of the modern age in architecture is the absence of visible symbols: we no longer seek on the surface that which we can obtain effectively only through penetration and participation in the function of a structure." If we put it in the words of Levi-Strauss, we can say that Hertzberger was searching for the precarious balance between Structure and Event. The open structure (like the grid) is not a designing tool, a device which is underneath the design process and pulled away at the end. The structure remains recognizable and apparent. In the tradition of the French architect Henri Labrouste, the structure of the plan is the essential generator of architecture and incites freedom, accommodating the unexpected and leading to a richer collective life. Hertzberger has never stopped professing that the distinction between "competence" (a form's potential for interpretation) and "performance" (how it is interpreted in a given situation and time) is an essential part of structuralism. Centraal Beheer has been considered the only "masterpiece" of Dutch architecture in the seventies.

Contemporary to Centraal Beheer are a couple of housing experiments of which only the "Diagoon" houses in Delft were realized. The basic idea was similar, but instead of the tight clustering and the "landscape of roof terraces", the blocks are linked to chains, with an interchanging of front and back of the dwellings. The decision of how to divide the space and how to use it is left to the occupants themselves. This principle has been pushed fur-

kann.» Die Anordnung in Halbgeschossen um ein Zentrum bot die Möglichkeit, zahlreiche diagonale Blickachsen zu schaffen. Zur ästhetischen Qualität tragen die Wandscheiben bei, die in Höhe und Breite differieren und allein durch die planimetrische Gegenüberstellung eine harmonische Wirkung schaffen. Mit diesem Wohnbaukonzept bemühte sich der Architekt um eine Alternative zur dogmatischen Funktionalität des traditionellen niederländischen Wohnbaus, wo mit dem Grundriß zugleich alle weiteren Möglichkeiten festgelegt sind.

Zwar hatte Hertzberger versucht, mit dem Entwurf für Centraal Beheer auch urbanistische Aspekte zu berücksichtigen, doch waren diese letzten Endes nicht klar genug gelöst, wofür sich zwei Gründe nennen lassen: Erstens fehlte dem von ihm zugrunde gelegten neutralen Rastersystem eine engere Beziehung zum städtischen Kontext sowie die Fähigkeit, optische Dominanten zu schaffen; zweitens blieb das Gebäude ein isoliertes Objekt, weil die Geschäfte, die in der Nachbarschaft entstehen sollten und das Bürohaus mit der Stadt verbunden hätten, nie gebaut wurden. Dieser Vorbehalt kann nicht für das Musikzentrum Vredenburg in Utrecht (1973–1978) gelten, das die Lücke zwischen der Altstadt, dem Einkaufszentrum Hoog Catharijne und dem Bahnhof schließt. Anders als das Einkaufszentrum weist Hertzbergers Bau menschliche Dimensionen auf, vor allem in den Stützen und in den überraschenden Ecken und Winkeln im Gebäudeinneren. Die ersten Entwürfe des Musikzentrums waren ambitiös; sie beruhten auf dem Prinzip von Kette und Einschlag. Die Kette als Garant für «die grundlegende Ordnung der Struktur … schafft aufgrund dieses Funktionsmerkmals zusammen mit dem Schuß die größtmögliche Vielfalt und Farbigkeit». In der späteren, vereinfachten Entwurfsfassung wurde auf dieses Prinzip weitgehend verzichtet. Statt Bauelemente zusammenzustellen, entschloß Hertzberger sich zur Entwicklung eines auf die Artikulation begründeten Ordnungssystems. Die Fassadenstützen und die freistehenden Stützen bilden ein Motiv, das in leicht abgewandelten Formen das ganze Gebäude durchzieht, und schaffen damit ein charakteristisches, unverwechselbares Bild. In seinen «Vorlesungen für Architekturstudenten» schrieb Hertzberger: «Die Ordnung der Stützen läßt sich als ein System verstehen, das Freiheit provoziert: als ‹Kompetenz›, die einen Anreiz für die an spezifische Situationen gebundene Performanz» schafft, und darum als Instrument, aus dem sich trotz Verzicht auf die Repetition von Räumen ein kohärentes Ordnungssystem ergab». Die Stütze als Definition von Ort und Raum wurde zum Hauptmerkmal einer «Handschrift». Auch wenn es hieß, in Vredenburg habe der Architekt seine strukturalen Komponenten so kombiniert, daß eine An-

ther in its manifestation. The houses are incomplete and offer through the incomplete framework a large number of possibilities for change and transformation. According to the architect, "the framework is a constant and represents, one might say, the order within which everybody's individual freedom and all freedoms together can be acted out and be contained." Many diagonal view lines have been created in the houses thanks to the split level disposition around a central core. An aesthetic quality is achieved thanks to the articulation of the wall in panels which, differing in height and breadth, present a harmony on the basis of purely planimetric juxtaposition. With these houses the architect tried to come to a solution for the dogmatic functionalist Dutch housing tradition, where everything has been determined once the floorplans are designed.

Although Hertzberger tried to give urbanistic implications to the office building of Centraal Beheer, these were, in the end, not very clear. Partly, because he established a neutral grid which didn't really interact with the existing urban tissue and didn't provide visual dominants; partly because the building remained an isolated object and the shops which were planned in the neighborhood and would have linked the building to the city were never built. The same cannot be said for the Music Center Vredenburg in Utrecht (1973–1978). The building has been used to bridge the gap between the old city, the Hoog Catharijne Shopping Center and the train station. In contrast to the shopping center, the work of Hertzberger shows human measure, especially in the columns and the surprising corners and angles inside the building.

The first plans of the music center were ambitious and showed the principle of warp and weft. The warp had to establish "the basic ordering of the fabric, and in doing that, create(s) the greatest possible variety and colourfulness with the weft". Later, in the reduced version, this principle was largely abandoned. Instead of mounting building elements, Hertzberger chose to develop a building order related to the principle of articulation. The columns in the facade and the freestanding columns constituted a motif which reoccurred in different variations throughout the building, and which therefore yielded a recognizable and characteristic image. As Hertzberger wrote in his Lessons for Students in Architecture: "The column structure may be seen as a system that generates freedom: a "competence" that provides an incentive for the "performance" belonging to a specific situation, and therefore, an instrument that yielded a coherent building order despite the absence of repetitive spaces". The column as a definition of place and space became the main ingredient of a "handwriting". Even if it has been said

sicht mit urbanem Charakter entstanden sei, sind sich Hertzberger und andere darüber im klaren, daß der Bau die Erwartungen, die man an ein autonomes Gebäude stellt, nicht unbedingt erfüllt. Die Baugeschichte war stark von Konflikten bestimmt, die ihre Spuren am Endprodukt hinterlassen haben. Das Ziel, einen einzigen weitläufigen Raum für die Konzerte zu schaffen, an dessen Peripherie ein Gang und kleinere Einheiten eine offene Beziehung zwischen Innen und Außen erlauben sollten, verursachte Reibungen zwischen Proportionierung und Größe. Das Stützensystem ließ im Inneren einen «plan libre» entstehen, die fortgesetzte Ausdifferenzierung von «Orten» führte jedoch zu einer labyrinthischen Raumentwicklung. Das Gebäude hat keine definitive Außenseite, und seine Erschließung führte schließlich, wie Hertzberger einräumte, «zu Lösungen an der Peripherie, die sich aus vielen Facetten zusammensetzt. Und weil alle diese Facetten dasselbe Material aufweisen, sind sie … nur Aspekte derselben Struktur. Mit anderen Worten, die Lesbarkeit der Teile ist stärker betont als die Lesbarkeit des Ganzen». Wohl ist der Bau ein Ausdruck der Demokratisierung der Gesellschaft und des Verzichts auf hierarchische Werte und zwar in einem Moment, als die niederländische Städtebaupolitik heftige Proteste auslöste; er blieb indes eigentümlich konturlos und wurde als Stoff, der ausfranst, oder als «Gewebe ohne Saum» beschrieben. Die im Inneren liegenden Gänge und gedeckten Wege sind voller Betriebsamkeit, mehr noch: die rauhe «Haut» des Gebäudes gibt ihm den Anschein, die Stadt könne ihm unmittelbar auf den Leib rücken und fugenlos mit ihm verschmelzen. Auch das Glas in den Fassaden gestattet eine leichte visuelle Osmose zwischen verschiedenen Zonen der Stadt: Es ist die durchlässige Oberfläche der Stadt.

Das strukturale Ordnungssystem wurde zum Hauptthema im Denken und in der Architektur Hertzbergers. 1970, in der Zeit der Studentenrevolten und Reformen im Unterrichtswesen, wurde er zum Ordinarius an der Technischen Universität Delft ernannt. In seinen Vorlesungen sprach er häufig von seiner Begeisterung für den Strukturalismus und die strukturale Linguistik und suchte wiederholt zu zeigen, wie sich gewisse Vorstellungen dieses neuen Denkansatzes in die Architektur «übertragen» ließen. Das neu thematisierte Problem der Sprache war die adäquate Antwort auf die Krise der Architektursprache der Moderne. Hertzbergers Werk macht deutlich, daß er weniger an den semantischen Qualitäten als an der Syntax des Bauens interessiert war; es ist alles getan, um den Charakter eines klar und deutlich artikulierten Zeichens auszulöschen. Als Lehrer machte Hertzberger den Unterschied zwischen dem kollektiven System von Zeichen, «langue», und der individuellen «parole». In Begriffen der Architek-

that in Vredenburg the architect combined his structural components in such a way to generate an urban elevation, both he and others are aware that it does not exactly live up to one's expectations concerning a self-contained building. Conflicts determined the building history, and these conflicts left their traces in the end product. The making of one large unified room for the music performances and creating a passage and smaller units around it, which would allow an open relation between inside and outside, caused some friction in the use of scale and size. The column system created a "plan libre" inside, but the continuous differentiation of "places" led to a labyrinthic spatial development. The building has no definitive outside and the accessibility – as Hertzberger admitted – "resulted in a peripheral arrangement composed of many facets and, because all these facets were built up of the same material, they are … merely many aspects of the same structure. In other words, more emphasis has been put on the legibility of the parts than of the whole." It implies a statement of the democratization of society and the loss of hierarchical values at a moment when Dutch urban politics were encountering major protest; as a building it is non distinctive and has been described as a fabric which unravels or "a tissue without a hem." Not only are the inside passages or covered alleys busy with incidents; the rough "skin" of the building gave it the appearance that the city could attach itself to it and incorporate it totally. Also, the glass in the facades permitted an easy visual osmoses between different zones of the city. It is the permeable surface of the city.

The building order became a major issue in the thinking and architecture of Hertzberger. In 1970, during the students democratization revolts and educational reforms, he was appointed to a professorship at the Technical University in Delft. In his lessons he often expressed his fascination with structuralism and linguistics and made various efforts of showing how certain concepts could be "translated" into architecture. The emergence of linguistics was a precise answer to the language crisis of modern architecture. It is evident from his work that Hertzberger was not so much interested in the semantic qualities of architecture as in the syntax. Everything has been done to eliminate the character of a clear and well defined sign. In his teaching, Hertzberger made a distinction between the collective "langue" and the individual "parole". In architectural terms: he was searching for a polyvalent form which would provoke individual interpretation. At the same time, as the Dutch architectural critic Hans van Dijk noted in 1979, his buildings "function as ‹dimostrazioni› of a very special translation of humanist values into architectural form." As is obvious from his

tur ausgedrückt: Er suchte nach einer polyvalenten Form, die individuelle Deutungen provozierte. Gleichzeitig sind seine Gebäude, wie der niederländische Architekturkritiker Hans van Dijk 1979 bemerkte, «dimostrazioni» einer ganz eigenen Übersetzung von humanistischen Werten in architektonische Form». Unübersehbar schreibt Hertzberger seine Architektur laufend um: sie wird zu einem Labor, in dem seine Ideen einen andauernden Bearbeitungsprozeß durchlaufen. So begann ein gründlicher und geduldiger Forschungsprozeß, der von den Ideen so unterschiedlicher Denker wie Sartre, Bachelard, Chomsky, Buber, Merleau-Ponty, Mitscherlich und Lévi-Strauss beeinflußt wurde und der ihn zu seiner eigenen Gestaltungsmethode führte, in deren Mittelpunkt die Themen der Nutzung und der Veränderung stehen. Immer wieder betonte er, daß ein Gebäude zum Wandel und zur Erneuerung fähig sein müsse, wenn solches in Zukunft erforderlich werde. Der Architekt solle darauf verzichten, die Nutzung eines Bauprogramms vorzuschreiben oder sich an dessen Rahmen zu halten, und statt dessen sein Bemühen vielmehr darauf richten, durch die Schaffung von Räumen, die sich von jedem Benutzer temporär in Gebrauch nehmen lassen, ein intensiveres und bewußteres Sozialverhalten zu fördern.

Ein anderer Begriff in Hertzbergers Schriften – er wird allerdings eher im negativen Sinn gebraucht – ist die Idee der Stadt. Die Reaktion auf die Stadt der Gegenwart fällt harsch aus, ihre feindselig-abweisende Glätte wird hart kritisiert. 1964 schreibt Hertzberger: «Die erste Stufe der beginnenden Einfriedung ist der Widerstand von Decken und Wänden; dieser Widerstand gibt Anlaß zur Verlangsamung oder Beschleunigung, er hat die Kraft, den Lebensrhythmus zu beeinflussen. Stadt – das heißt die Umgebung zur Einzäunung machen». Die rauhe Unebenheit der Betonsteine spielt auf die Tatsache an, daß ein Gebäude nie vollendet ist, sondern dank seiner Deutung und Nutzung durch die Menschen ein Eigenleben hat. Die von Hertzberger geschaffenen Gelegenheiten für eine plurale Nutzung, sollen dieses Eigenleben stimulieren.

Die Krönung von Hertzbergers strukturalistischer Architektur ist das Bürohaus des Ministeriums für Arbeit und Soziales (1979–1990). 1979 erhielt Hertzberger den Auftrag, an der Hauptbahnlinie Amsterdam–Rotterdam «ein offenes und kommunikatives» Gebäude mit einer angenehmen Arbeitsplatzatmosphäre für etwa 2000 Staatsdiener zu schaffen. Budgetkürzungen und neue Anforderungen zwangen den Architekten dazu, seinen ersten Vorschlag mehrmals zu überarbeiten. Das Resultat ist ein Gebäude – eine «freundliche Burg», wie Hertzberger es nannte –, das sich aus sechzehn eng benachbarten oktagonalen Türmen zusammensetzt, die durch Galerien ver-

works, Hertzberger continuously writes and rewrites his architecture, making it into a laboratory in which his ideas are constantly elaborated. A thorough and patient research began, whereby he was influenced by ideas of heterogene thinkers like Sartre, Bachelard, Chomsky, Buber, Merleau-Ponty, Mitscherlich and Levi-Strauss, leading to his own design-approach in which the issues of the use and change of the building are central. He often emphasized that a building should be capable of adaption and upgrading when required. An architect should not prescribe the use nor stick to the limits of the building program. Instead, he should try to stimulate a more intense and conscious social behavior, creating spaces which can be temporarily appropriated.

Another concept which we encounter in his writings, even if it is in a rather negative sense, is the idea of a town. The reaction towards the contemporary town is harsh; the smoothness and hostility are criticized severely. Hertzberger wrote in 1964: "The first stage in the formation of enclosure is the resistance of floor and wall; it is this resistance which causes one to slow down or accelerate, which can influence the rhythm of existence: i.e. the forming of our surroundings into enclosure; town." The roughness of the concrete brick alludes to the fact that a building is never finished but has a life of its own due to the interpretations and the use of the people. In order to stimulate this, he created many opportunities for pluralistic use.

The apotheoses of his structuralistic architecture is to be found in the office building for the Ministry of Social Welfare (1979–1990). In 1979, Hertzberger was commissioned to design "an open and communicative" building along the main railway line from Amsterdam to Rotterdam. It was meant to be a well-tempered environment for about 2000 civil servants. Due to a reduced budget and new requirements, the architect had to change his first proposal several times. The end result is a building, a "friendly castle" as Hertzberger called it, composed of sixteen octagonal towers which are tightly clustered, linked by galleries and grouped around a continuous inner street or interior courtyards. The main entry is set centrally in the symmetrical south facade that faces the railway. Comparing it with Centraal Beheer, Peter Buchanan writes enthusiastically about this "Beheer's Big Brother" in 1991 and says that "…by now Hertzberger's structuralist approach has evolved far beyond the simple repetition of standard elements to being a sophisticated syntax that disciplines whole families of related but varied elements and junction conditions. … he has moved beyond rhythmic reiteration of the same words to stringing complex sentences together and, in place of the homoge-

bunden sind und sich um eine durchlaufende Binnenstraße oder um Innenhöfe gruppieren. Der Haupteingang ist in die Mitte der symmetrisch gestalteten, den Gleisen zugewandten Südfassade gesetzt. Peter Buchanan verglich das Gebäude mit Centraal Beheer und schrieb 1991 voller Begeisterung über «Beheers Big Brother»: «Hertzbergers strukturalistischer Ansatz hat die simple Wiederholung von Standardelementen weit hinter sich gelassen und sich zu einer differenzierten Syntax entwickelt, die ganze Familien von verwandten, doch vielfältigen Elementen und Anschlußmöglichkeiten diszipliniert. (…) Aus der rhythmischen Wiederholung derselben Wörter sind Ketten komplexer Sätze geworden, und an die Stelle des homogen kumulativen Charakters von Centraal Beheer ist eine subtil ausgefeilte, hierarchische Gestaltung getreten, die größere organisatorische Flexibilität erlaubt und noch reichere Möglichkeiten der internen Kommunikation verspricht».

Obwohl Buchanan das Ministerium als zukunftsträchtiges Werk betrachtet, ist mit dieser Arbeit unübersehbar ein Wendepunkt in Hertzbergers Schaffen erreicht. Der Architekt machte zwar auch weiterhin vom Prinzip der verbundenen Türme beim Bau von Bürogebäuden Gebrauch – in den Aufträgen für Gruner & Jahr in Hamburg (1983), für die Stadtwerke in Frankfurt a. M. (1985) und für Schering in Berlin (1988). Doch obwohl er seine alten Steckenpferde nicht endgültig aufgab, hatte sich Hertzberger am Ende des zehnjährigen Entwurfs- und Bauprozesses seines Ministeriums für Arbeit und Soziales doch in verschiedene Richtungen weiterentwickelt und experimentierte nun an neuen Fronten.

Um nicht zum Propheten entbehrlicher, abgedroschener oder belehrender Botschaften zu werden – eine Gefahr, deren er sich wohl bewußt war –, bemühte er sich um ein Verständnis für den beginnenden sozialen Gesinnungswandel. Dem ideologischen Kampfplatz der sechziger und siebziger Jahre mit seinen Überresten von Unschuld und Hoffnung hatte man den Rücken gekehrt, die soziale Verantwortung der Architektur verlor im Zuge dieses Wandels an Bedeutung, eine Rückkehr zur Fachdisziplin und zu fachimmanenten Fragen bahnte sich an. Hertzberger war jedoch besonnen genug, sich in seiner eigenen Arbeit vom Ideenpool der Postmoderne fernzuhalten, die sich als Revision der Moderne und als reiner Ästhetizismus in Szene setzte. Mit einer gewissen Neugier verfolgte er die Aktivitäten seiner Kollegen. Gelegenheit dazu boten die zahlreichen internationalen Wettbewerbe, zu denen er eingeladen war – vor allem in Deutschland, wo nach 1982, dem Jahr der Wahl Helmut Kohls zum Bundeskanzler, neokonservative Strömungen wieder auflebten. Statt die neuen Trends von vornherein abzulehnen und zu verur-

Oaxaca, Mexico, 1996

neously cumulative character of Centraal Beheer, he has created a subtly elaborated and hierarchic design that offers greater flexibility in organization and even richer vision of internal community." Although he sees the Ministry as a seminal building, it marks a point of change in the work of Hertzberger. The architect still used the same principle of interlinking "towers" in projects for office buildings, like those for Gruner & Jahr in Hamburg (1983), Stadtwerke in Frankfurt a.M. (1985) and Schering in Berlin (1988), but at the end of ten years of the design and building process of the Ministry of Social Welfare Hertzberger had evolved in different directions and was experimenting on other fronts without giving up all his old "hobby-horses".

Aware of the danger of broadcasting superfluous, rhetorical or exhortative messages, he felt that he had to keep "in tune" with the changing mentality. The ideological battleground of the sixties and seventies, covered with the remains of innocence and hope, lay behind everybody. The change which occurred reduced the importance of the social value of architecture. It led to a return to the professional discipline and its immanent problems. In his own work, Hertzberger was, nevertheless, always careful enough to stay out of the pool of post-modernism, which was promoted as a revision of the modern, and pure aestheticism. With a certain curiosity he confronted himself with what his colleagues were doing. Broad occasion was given to him in the many international competitions for

teilen, zeigte sich Hertzberger aufgeschlossen und gewann durch seine wachsende Toleranz eine neue Freiheit und ein reicheres «poetisches» Vokabular. Sein Werk nach 1986 zeigt, daß er sich neue Quellen erschloß und gleichzeitig von alten Ideen distanzierte.

In der Seniorenwohnanlage in Almere Haven und in den Amsterdamer Apolloschulen sind noch Spuren des Ordnungssystems zu erkennen. Beide Schulen lassen an städtische Villen denken; doch die Einfachheit des kompakten Entwurfs mit seiner leicht palladianischen Attitüde täuscht: Der Schnitt gibt zu erkennen, wie durch die versetzte Geschoßanordnung der Klassenzimmer um das zentrale Foyer eine ungewöhnlich interessante, reich artikulierte Gestaltung entstanden ist. Die Treppen und Treppenabsätze sind multifunktional; sie erschließen nicht nur die Klassenzimmer, sondern dienen darüber hinaus als Sitze und Galerien, wenn die Halle für Gemeinschaftsveranstaltungen genutzt wird, und bieten den Kindern Platz zum Sitzen, Spielen oder für individuelles Arbeiten. Sie sind Übergangszonen zwischen Klasse und Schulgebäude. Der Entwurf solcher Zwischen-Räume nimmt in Hertzbergers Schaffen eine bevorzugte Stellung ein. Sie werden als Zonen aufgefaßt, in denen sich öffentlicher und privater Bereich begegnen. Das wird nicht nur in den zahlreichen Schulgebäuden Hertzbergers anschaulich, sondern auch in den Projekten für Kassel und für die Haarlemmer Houttuinen, in denen die Treppenhäuser «eine wichtigere Rolle spielen als die Wohnungen selbst». In Kassel sind die Treppen zu Gliedern einer Kette geworden, während sie in den Haarlemmer Houttuinen nach außen hervortreten und den Sockel für Balkone mit Blick auf die ruhige Straße bilden. Die Schulen sind als «winzige Städte in sich» aufgefaßt. Immer sind die Klassen um eine gemeinsame Straße oder platzartige Halle angeordnet. Form und Organisation der Räume sollen spontane und organisierte Kontakte anregen.

Einen anderen Ansatz zeigt der Entwurf für das Berliner Filmzentrum Esplanade (1986), ein Konglomerat getrennter Gebäudeeinheiten, die durch überdachte, galerieähnliche Passerellen verbunden sind. Auch hier spricht Hertzberger noch von einem Ordnungssystem. Es handelt sich jedoch um ein System neuen Typs. Die einzelnen Komponenten setzen sich aus identischen Raumelementen zusammen, die aufgrund ihres Ordnungssystems ein einheitliches Ganzes bilden. Dasselbe Prinzip liegt dem Entwurf für den Bicocca-Wettbewerb zugrunde. Der Vorschlag des Architekten sieht im wesentlichen vor, ein Grundmuster, ein System von Gebäudereihen, zu erstellen. Bezeichnenderweise bezieht sich Hertzberger in seinem Projekt auf ein Gemälde von Giorgio Morandi, eine Gruppe runder Objekte, die nebeneinander plaziert sind – Hinweis

which he was invited, especially in Germany, a country that was afflicted by a neo-conservative tendency after 1982 when Helmut Kohl became prime minister. Instead of rejecting and fulminating a priori against certain trends, his increasing tolerance brought him a new freedom and a richer poetic vocabulary. He tapped into new sources and took his distance from others. This becomes apparent in his work after 1986.

Traces of the building order can still be found in the residential building for elderly people in Almere Haven or the two Apollo Schools at Amsterdam. Both schools look like urban villas. The simplicity of the compact plan with its Palladian touch is deceptive, mainly because in section the split-level arrangement of the classrooms around the central hall makes it into particularly interesting and richly articulated buildings. The different stairs and landings are multi-functional: in addition to leading to the classrooms they serve as seats and galleries when the central hall is used for a collective event and they contain places where the children can sit, play or have a more private area to work. They are the transitional zones from the school to the classroom.

Designing the in-between spaces has been a favorite theme in the work of Hertzberger. Always, these spaces have been conceived as the zone where the public meets the private and visa versa. This is not only apparent in the many schools that Hertzberger has designed, but also in the projects for Kassel and the Haarlemmer Houttuinen where the communal staircases "play a more focal role than the actual dwellings." In Kassel, the staircases have become links in a chain, whereas in the Haarlemmer Houttuinen they protrude towards the outside and form the foundation for balconies that look out over the quiet street. The schools are considered as "tiny self-sufficient cities." Always, the classrooms have been distributed around a common street or square hall. The shape and organization of the space incites spontaneous and organized contacts. A different approach has been taken in the project for the Film Center "Esplanade" in Berlin (1986). This building was conceived as a conglomerate of separate building units, connected by covered, gallery-like walkways. In this project, Hertzberger still talks of a building order, but it is of a different kind. The individual components are constituted by the same spatial elements which combine, as a building order, to form a unified whole. The same principle can be found in the project for the Bicocca competition. Mainly, the architect opted for establishing a pattern; a system of building alignments. It is revealing that Hertzberger refers in this project to a painting from Giorgio Morandi with a pair of round ob-

auf eine andere Organisation von Formen im Raum und auf die Verwandtschaft zwischen den isolierten Einzelformen. In dieser Zeit verwendet der Architekt vorzugsweise runde Formen, aus denen Segmente entfernt oder ausgeschnitten sind. Bildlich gesprochen: die perfekte, in sich abgeschlossene Form wird verletzlich gemacht. Das wird besonders deutlich am Gebäude des Theaterzentrums Spui in Den Haag, das vom Amphitheater angeregt ist, einem der baulichen Archetypen, denen Hertzbergers besondere Vorliebe gilt. Der Bau ist jedoch kein in sich geschlossenes Zeichen, das sich selbst genügt; er tritt vielmehr entschlossen in Dialog mit seiner Umgebung. Seine urbane Form, die bei der Annäherung die verschiedenen Blickachsen berücksichtigt, läßt sich als Reaktion auf die besondere Lage des Gebäudes erkennen, die seine urbane Funktion verstärkt. Um eine maximale Erschließung des Gebäudes zu erreichen, hat der Architekt die Straße einbezogen, die das Gebäude wie ein Keil spaltet und es auf den davorliegenden Platz hin öffnet. Auf diese Weise wird eine Verlängerung des Foyers und des öffentlichen Bereichs im Außenraum erreicht. Der Eingangsbereich präsentiert sich als Zone, in der sich verschiedene Baukörper, einander kontrastierend, überschneiden.

Nach 1989 richtete Hertzberger seine Aufmerksamkeit vermehrt auf die Wirkung der baulichen Form. Zu dieser neuen Einstellung dürfte seine Funktion als Leiter des Berlage Instituts beigetragen haben, das sich zum Ziel setzte, werdenden Architekten ein Nachdiplomstudium anzubieten, das höchsten internationalen Ansprüchen gerecht wird. Er wirkte nicht nur als Lehrer, sondern lernte seinerseits von den Studierenden, deren «Input» er bewunderte. Er erkannte, was nach dem Fall der Berliner Mauer jedermann deutlich wurde: daß jede dogmatische Position negative Folgen hat. Zwar blieb er weiterhin dem Glauben verpflichtet, den Bakema und van Eyck 1962 formulierten, daß «die Architektur eine Funktion sein könnte, die das Recht eines jeden auf ein unversehrtes Leben verwirklicht». Er war sich jedoch darüber im klaren, daß neue Vorstellungen und Eigenarten der Gegenwart aufgenommen und transformiert werden mußten. «Uns interessieren in erster Linie neue Beispiele der Architektur, die zu einer besseren Raumgestaltung anregen, die den Horizont menschlicher Erfahrung erweitern, die besser funktionieren und mehr Ausdruckskraft haben, die erfrischend und, wer weiß, vielleicht auch schön sind», schreibt er in der ersten Nummer der Berlage Cahiers. Sein begrenztes Interesse für intellektuelle Deutungen und Verfahren hinderte ihn nicht daran, sich von den Auffassungen eines Rem Koolhaas faszinieren und begeistern zu lassen, den er häufig als Gastdozent ans Berlage Institut holte.

jects placed beside each other. It is an indication of a different organization of forms in space and the relationship between these single, isolated forms. At the time, the architect shows a particular interest in the use of round forms, of which segments have been removed or cut out. Metaphorically speaking, the perfect, concluded form has been rendered vulnerable. This is especially clear in the building of the Theater Center Spui in The Hague which is inspired by one of the archetypes of which Hertzberger is fond: the amphitheater. The building is, however, not a self indulgent sign, contained in itself, but deliberately opens up a dialogue with its surroundings. In the urban form, which takes into regard the different sight lines when approaching the building, we can detect a reaction to its specific location which gives the Theater Center a more pronounced urban function. In order to make the building more accessible, the architect has pulled in the street, which splits the building like a wedge and opens it to the square in front. Thus, a continuation of the foyer area and the public realm outside of the building is achieved. The entry zone is the place where different building volumes intersect and contrast with each other.

After 1989 Hertzberger began dedicating more attention to the impact of the architectural form. Being chairman of the Berlage Institute, which aspired to be an international top ranking postgraduate architectural school, certainly contributed to this new outlook. He was not only teaching but also learning from the different students and admiring their "input". He learned, as became clear to everyone after the fall of the Berlin wall, that any dogmatic position has negative effects. Even if he still believed, as did Bakema and Van Eyck in 1962, that "architecture could be a function realizing everybody's right to full life," he was aware that new concepts and characteristics of our time had to be used and transformed. "What we are, above all, interested in – he writes in the first Berlage Cahier – are new examples of architecture which offer stimuli for the creation of better spatial organizations, which will expand the horizon of human experience, function better, have more expressive force; which will be refreshing and perhaps, who knows, beautiful." Even if Hertzberger doesn't show a great interest for intellectual interpretations and procedures, he was, nevertheless, intrigued and stimulated by the views of Rem Koolhaas, who he often invited to teach at the Berlage Institute.

In the extension to the primary school at Aerdenhout (1988–1989) we also find a contrasting relationship between forms. There is the two story rectangular classroom block of white concrete bricks, which is aligned with the

Eine Kontrastbeziehung – zwischen Formen – finden wir auch in der Erweiterung der Grundschule in Aerdenhout (1988–1989). Da ist einmal der zweigeschossige Rechteckblock mit Klassenzimmern aus weißen Betonsteinen, der sich formal an die dahinterliegenden Wohnbauten anschließt. Ihm ist der Schirm des gekrümmten schwarzen Blocks mit Klassenzimmern vorangestellt, der die Bewegung der benachbarten Straße aufnimmt. Das Foyer ist keilförmig zwischen die zwei Blöcke gesetzt. Die dynamische Beziehung zwischen den Teilen des Erweiterungsbaus ist nicht durch eine repetitiv-geometrische strukturelle Strenge bestimmt, sondern durch das fortschreitende Eingehen auf die urbanen Gegebenheiten. Der Unterschied wird auch an den verwendeten Materialien deutlich. Viele Kritiker sehen in Hertzbergers Arbeiten seit 1990, namentlich in der Hinwendung zu einem stärkeren visuellen Ausdruck nach außen, eine Abkehr von der strukturalistischen Methode. Das trifft jedoch nur teilweise zu. Erst vor kurzem hat der Architekt seine Auffassung unterstrichen, daß der Strukturalismus «seine Kraft aus dem Paradox bezieht, daß Ordnung, durch die Vorgabe des geeigneten strukturalen Themas, Freiheit weniger einschränkt, als vielmehr Freiheit provoziert, weil sie Raum für Unverhofftes läßt». Sein wesentliches Anliegen ist weiterhin die Organisation des Raums und nicht die Fassadengestaltung.

Das Projekt für den Kölner Medienpark (1990) ist der Versuch, das gängige Verfahren zur Ausfüllung eines Blockgevierts zu ändern. Statt das Binnengelände wie üblich durch Blockbauten nach außen abzuschließen, richtet Hertzberger die Bauten nach innen aus und schafft dadurch einen öffentlichen Bereich. Wieder ist die Stadt in den Baukomplex hineingenommen. Die nach innen weisenden Gebäuderückseiten werden zu Vorderfronten. In gewisser Weise ist die Grundidee eine Weiterführung und Entwicklung von Vorstellungen, die bereits die Moderne beschäftigten. Hertzbergers Entwurf für den Medienpark scheint von den um 1920 entstandenen Wolkenkratzer-Projekten Mies van der Rohes inspiriert. Wie Mies versucht Hertzberger die Bestimmung des Gebäudes so weit wie möglich offenzulassen. Eine andere Form der Weiterverarbeitung von Konzepten der Moderne findet sich in den Dürener Wohnbauten und im Städtebauentwurf Middelburg (1995), wo unterschiedliche Haustypen unter einem durchgezogenen Dach zu einer Hofrandbebauung zusammengefaßt sind. Das Konzept breiter Galerien rings um den Innenhof, in denen Kinder spielen können, gehört zum Bestand von Hertzbergers Musée imaginaire, seiner persönlichen Bibliothek von Bildsymbolen. Das Vorbild war der von Hertzberger bewunderte Spangen-Komplex in Rotterdam, ein Entwurf Michiel Brinkmans aus dem

Santorini, Greece, 1996

domestic buildings behind. The black, curved front block of classrooms forms a screen that follows the movement of the nearby road. The hall is placed between these two blocks like a wedge. The dynamic relationship between the parts of the extension has not been determined by a geometric and repetitive structuralist rigor, but by a progressive reacting to the urban setting. The contrast is also noticeable in the materials which he used. Many critics have interpreted Hertzbergers work since 1990 and, in the first place, the shift towards a greater visual expression in the exterior as a move away from the structuralist approach. This is only partly true. The architect has recently stressed again that in his view structuralism "is nurtured on the paradox that order, rather than limiting freedom by using the correct structural theme, in fact incites freedom, making space for the unexpected." The main question for him remains the organization of space and not the creation of facades.

The project for the MediaPark in Cologne (1990) is an attempt to change the customary "modus operandi" of filling in a city block. Instead of closing off the private compound area with building blocks, Hertzberger makes a public area out of this space by bending the buildings towards the inside. Again, the city is pulled in. The inside-looking rear facades become front facades. In a way, the underlying idea is a continuation and elaboration of concepts which modernists tried to tackle. In plan, the Media-

Jahr 1919. Dieser Entwurfsidee wurden jedoch, vor allem im Plan für Middelburg, andere Konzepte mit dem Ziel zur Seite gestellt, neue Lösungen für städtische Siedlungsräume zu schaffen. In Middelburg wurde die landläufige Anordnung umgekehrt: Das Blockinnere, der Hof, gehört zum öffentlichen Raum, während Gärten und Parks an die Außenseite gelegt sind.

Hertzbergers letzter größerer Bauauftrag ist das Chassé-Theater in Breda (1992–1995). Er führt in dieser Arbeit, wie gleichzeitig Richard Rogers in seinem Entwurf für den Flughafen Heathrow, das Thema der dynamisch gekrümmten Dachfläche ein, die das Gebäude wie eine in zwei Stücke gerissene Decke überzieht. Das Dach als Landschaft gehörte zwar schon zu den Themen der Gruppe Forum; doch hatte man es nie als neue expressive Kraft verstanden. Die Vorstellung des Daches als einer optischen Dominante war obsolet. Die meisten «Forum»-Mitglieder standen den steilen Dächern, die zum Inventar der traditionellen Bauweise der Delfter Schule gehörten, mit ausgesprochener Abneigung gegenüber. Die Bedeutung des neuen Motivs wird wie folgt beschrieben: «Die Doppelwelle des Daches, die über die zwei Bühnentürme spült und dann auf den Foyerbereich herabfällt, soll vor allem bewirken, daß keine einzelne Komponente sich als dominierendes Element hervortut. Diese Funktion – alle Elemente des Gebäudes zusammenzufassen – macht die Dächer zur eigentlichen Fassade». Das Raumresiduum zwischen den Baukörpern ist als Foyer genutzt, das weit ins Gebäude hineinreicht. Die Glasfassaden, Laufbrücken und Treppen im Foyerbereich schaffen die Voraussetzung dafür, daß die Besucher des Hauses «sehen und gesehen werden». Mit dem gewellten Dach wird in der Stadt ein «natürliches» optisches Zeichen gesetzt. In einer Skulptur von Alberto Giacometti, «Femme couchée qui rêve» aus dem Jahr 1929, die den Körper der Frau durch Kraftlinien andeutet, sieht Hertzberger das Vorbild dieser neuen Metapher, die darauf zielt, unsere Lebenskultur zu verändern und dadurch den Umgang des Menschen mit seiner Umgebung zu beeinflussen. Da das Auge fortwährend aktiv gehalten wird, ist in diesem Theaterbau auch das Thema Bewegung und Geschwindigkeit aufgenommen.

Nur ein kleiner Schritt führt vom Chassé-Theater zu neueren Projekten wie Clemensänger in Freising (1993), dem Auditorium in Rom (1993) oder dem Potsdamer Landtagsgebäude (1995), in denen das Dach ebenfalls eine vorherrschende Rolle spielt. In diesen Arbeiten, die die Bedeutung der Architektur für die Umwelt unter neuen Gesichtspunkten thematisieren, wird das Dach zu einer Erweiterung der Landschaft. Die Gebäude treten nicht mehr als selbständige Gebilde hervor, die die Landschaft dominieren, sondern sind versenkt. Mutter Erde ist durch

Park seems to be inspired by the skyscraper projects of Mies van der Rohe around 1920. Like Mies, Hertzberger tries to leave the destination of the building as open as possible. A different kind of reworking of modernist concepts can be found in the housing complex in Düren and the urban scheme in Middelburg (1995) where the architect has put different housing types in one block and underneath one continuous roof. The concept of wide galleries around the inner courtyard, which form an upper street where kids can play, belongs to the "musée imaginaire" of Hertzberger, his personal library of images; he derived it from the Spangen complex in Rotterdam that M. Brinkman designed in 1919 and for which Hertzberger always had a great admiration. But this concept is combined with others, especially in Middelburg, in order to come to new solutions for urban settlements. In Middelburg, the typical situation has been turned around. The inside, the courtyard of the blocks belongs to the urban space, whereas the outside has become gardens and a public park.

The Chassé Theater in Breda (1992–1995) is his latest major built work. In this building he introduced, as did Richard Rogers at the same time in his project for the Heathrow Airport, the theme of the dynamically curved roof, which covers the building like a torn blanket. The roof as a landscape had been one of the themes of the Forum group. But never was the roof considered as a new expressive force. The roof as image determinant had been abolished completely. Most Forum members showed a distaste of the steep roofs that were associated with the architecture of the traditional Delftse School. The importance of the new feature is the following: "The double wave of roof washing over the flytowers and cascading down over the foyer zone is there primarily to prevent any one component from dominating. The fact that the roofs pull together all the building's elements makes it the principal facade." Underneath the roof, the residual space between the built masses is used as a foyer which runs deep into the building. The glass facades, the bridges and stairs in the foyer zone take care that the visitors "can see and are seen" when they go to the events. With the waving of the roof, a more "natural" visual element has been brought into the city. Hertzberger sees in the sculpture of Alberto Giacometti "Femme couchée qui rêve", dating from 1929 where the body of the woman is indicated by force-lines, an inspiration for this new metaphor, which is meant to change the culture in which we live thereby affecting the ways in which humans interact with their environment. In the theater also, the theme of movement and speed is taken up in the sense that the eye is constantly held active.

Einschnitte geöffnet worden, und unter dem Dach der Erdoberfläche finden verschiedene Funktionen Raum: die Erde ist fruchtbar gemacht. Ein ähnliches Verfahren zeigen die Bilder von Lucio Fontana. Die Schnitte in seinen Leinwänden haben nichts Destruktives; sie sollen neue Horizonte erschließen.

In den jüngeren Arbeiten Hertzbergers ist diese Suche nach neuen Metaphern, die den bildhaften Ausdruck der Architektur erweitert, von besonderer Wichtigkeit. Vor kurzem sprach der Architekt vor einer großen Zuhörerschaft über seine Entwürfe für das Musicon in Bremen und bemerkte bei dieser Gelegenheit: «Ich ertrage Gebäude einfach nicht mehr, diese rechteckigen Kästen, die nichts als abgeschlossene Gegenstände sind, ich denke eher an Schiffe und Wellen … und hier steht die Vorstellung eines großen Schiffes im Vordergrund, in dem das Bauprogramm enthalten ist.» Diese Aussage ist weder als Plädoyer für einen formalistischen Ansatz zu werten, noch steht sie für einen Flirt mit Modetrends oder den Glauben an das perfekte Objekt. Vielmehr ist Hertzberger nach wie vor auf der Suche nach der flexiblen Form, der Form, die die größtmögliche Nutzungsvielfalt eines Gebäudes erlaubt und zugleich soziales Verhalten fördert und intensiviert. Auch wenn das Dach zur Hauptfassade geworden ist und damit als augenfälliges Element zu offensichtlicher Bedeutung gelangt, folgt die Raumordnung des Gebäudes unverändert den Prinzipien, die für Hertzberger seit je leitend waren. Die relative Unabhängigkeit des Daches ist durch eine verstärkte Aufmerksamkeit für die Tragkonstruktion kompensiert, die mit ihren Stützen noch immer Räume schafft.

So leidenschaftlich wie wohl kein anderer Architekt seiner Zeit hat Hertzberger in den vergangenen dreißig Jahren Bilder und Erfahrungen aufgenommen und gesammelt; die große Zahl seiner Skizzenbücher legt Zeugnis davon ab. In seinen Schriften nennt er ausdrücklich historische Beispiele aus verschiedenen Kulturen, die ihm als Anregung gedient haben. Ohne je versucht zu sein, sie einfach zu kopieren, benutzt er sie als Ausgangspunkt – als Inspiration und als Rohmaterial, das er in der Folge so weit ausarbeitet und umgestaltet, daß seine Konzepte, Ausgangspunkte und Ideen in dem Gebäude Raum finden. 1967, in der Zeit, als er sich mit utopischen Projekten wie der «Plug-in-City» beschäftigte, schrieb Peter Cook: «Da die Architektur eine soziale Kunst ist, liegt der Wert eines Gebäudes hauptsächlich in seiner Fähigkeit, aus menschlichen Situationen Milieus zu schaffen. Der Architekt kann sich, wenn er will, an das bestehende Schema halten. Ein Mehrfamilienhaus kann genau nach solchen Standards für Raum, Licht, Wohndichte und Atmosphäre entworfen

The step from the Chassé Theater to the recent projects like Clemensänger in Freising (1993), the Auditorium in Rome (1993) or the office building for the Landtag in Potsdam (1995), where the roof also plays a predominant role, is a small one. In these projects, where the issue of the environmental performance of architecture is brought into new directions, the roof has become an extension of landscape. The buildings do not stand out and dominate the landscape but are submerged. Mother Earth has been cut and serves as surface underneath which different functions can be placed. The earth is fertilized. We might look at the paintings of Lucio Fontana for a similar way of operation. The cuts he makes in his canvases are not made to destroy the work but to open up new horizons. This search for new metaphors, which enriches the figurative idiom of architecture, is very important in the recent works of Hertzberger. When explaining his plans of the Music Theater in Bremen (1995) to a large audience the architect recently said: "I just can't stand buildings anymore, rectangle ones which are just closed off objects. I think more of boats and waves … the idea here is that you have this big boat that contains the program." This should certainly not be conceived as a plea for a formalistic approach; nor is it a flirtation with the ephemera or a belief in the perfect object. On the contrary, Hertzberger still looks for the most flexible shape which permits the building to be used in many ways and which, at the same time, can arouse and intensify social behavior. Even if the roof as the main facade has gained an evident status as an eye catching element, the organization of the space in the building still follows the principles which Hertzberger has been advocating all along. The relative independence of the roof has been compensated by a greater attention to the supporting structure which, through its columns, still provides spaces.

Probably as no other architect of the last thirty years, Hertzberger has been an avid consumer and collector of images and experiences, as his large number of sketchbooks illustrate. In his writings he overtly refers to historical examples from various cultures as sources of inspiration, but he is never inclined to just copy them. Instead, he uses them as a point of departure, as thought stimulation, as raw material, which he subsequently elaborates and remodels in order that his concepts and ideas fit into the building. Peter Cook wrote in 1967, in the years that he was involved in utopian projects like the "Plug-in City": "As architecture is a social art, the value of a building must lie chiefly in its ability to create environment out of human situations. The architect can, if he wishes, set himself the limit of the existing pattern. A block of flats

werden, aber die meisten guten Architekten würden sich damit nicht begnügen.» Hertzberger, soviel ist sicher, hat sich nie damit begnügt. Er ist ständig auf der Suche nach neuen Lösungen und stellt frühere Lösungen zur Disposition, ohne dabei sein Engagement für die sozialen und öffentlichen Dimensionen der Architektur aufzugeben. Sein Werk vermittelt den Eindruck einer ungewöhnlichen Konsequenz und Kontinuität. Die letzten Jahre haben ihn aber auch zu der Einsicht gebracht, daß die Menschen visuelle Reize verlangen und brauchen und daß er stärker darauf zu achten habe, «in größeren Maßstäben» zu denken. Diese Erkenntnis hat ihm neue Wege gewiesen, Wege, die noch zu erschließen und zu entwickeln sind. Die Zukunft wird ihren Wert für ein Fach erweisen, das allen Bemühungen zum Trotz stärker von Substanzverlust und Beliebigkeit geprägt zu sein scheint als je zuvor.

can be designed with exactly those standards of space: light, density and atmosphere; but most good architects would not be content with this." Certainly, Hertzberger is never content with this. He is always looking for new solutions and re-elaborating old ones, without abandoning his commitment to the social and public dimension of architecture. He has produced an oeuvre which shows in its development an incredible consistency and continuity. But in the last years he has also become aware of the fact that people want and need visual excitement and that he had to have more attention for "the large scale". This has brought him onto new roads which are still in progress and process and which will show their fortune for the future of a discipline that, despite all efforts, seems more hollow and ruled by arbitrariness than ever before.

Bauten und Projekte   Buildings and Projects

Studentenheim
Amsterdam, 1959–1966

Student Housing
Amsterdam, 1959–1966

Eines der Hauptmerkmale des Gebäudes, dessen Entwurf als Wettbewerbsbeitrag eingereicht wurde, ist die besondere Führung des öffentlichen Bereichs: Er durchzieht das gesamte Haus und schafft sowohl einen Raum der Begegnung für die 250 Bewohner als auch eine Zone für die externen Benutzer der Einrichtungen im Erdgeschoß. Besonderen Wert legte man auf die Ausgestaltung der im vierten Stock gelegenen «Wohnstraße». Der Architekt hält fest: «Ein Gebäude kann durch den Entwurf noch so definitiv bestimmt sein, letzten Endes sind es die Bewohner, die nach der Übernahme weiter daran arbeiten, es ständig verändern und erneuern. Sie verstehen es auf ihre Art, und je mehr Ergänzungsmöglichkeiten der Plan zuläßt, desto mehr Menschen können sich darin heimisch fühlen. Je mehr unterschiedliche Identifikationsspuren ein Gebäude aufnehmen kann, desto leichter wird es zu einem Zuhause, dem jeder Bewohner ein anderes, individuelles Gepräge gibt. Architekten sollten lediglich die Wand schaffen, an die jeder schreiben kann, was er mitteilen möchte.» In seinem heutigen Zustand läßt das Gebäude allerdings kaum noch etwas von der subtilen Detailbehandlung erkennen, die einen Besuch in früherer Zeit zum Abenteuer der Architektur werden ließ.

One of the main features of this building, which was the result of a competition, is the way the public zone penetrates through the building and makes it into a special meeting place for the 250 students living there as well as a zone for those who want to use the facilities on the ground floor. Special attention was given to the "living street" on the fourth floor. The architect is of the opinion that "however far a designer takes a building, it is the occupants who go on making it after they have taken over, constantly changing and renewing. They interpret it in their own way, and the more diverse in which the building allows for completion, the more people can feel at home in it. The more differing marks of identification a building can obtain, the more it will be a home that every occupant makes into something else, something more of himself. What architects should make is the wall on which everyone can write whatever he wants to communicate." The building in its present state hardly illustrates the subtle detailing, which once made a visit an architectural adventure.

Küchenelement im Gemeinschaftsraum / Kitchen block in the communal area

Ansicht von Westen / View from the west

Wettbewerbsentwurf / Competition design

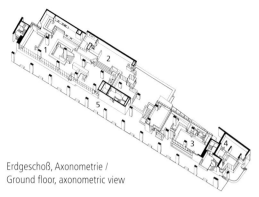

Erdgeschoß, Axonometrie /
Ground floor, axonometric view

|— 10 —|

Grundriß 5., 6., 7. Geschoß / Plan 5th, 6th, 7th floor
Grundriß 1., 2., 3. Geschoß / Plan 1st, 2nd, 3rd floor

1. Zentrales Treppenhaus / Central staircase
2. Vorraum / Lobby
3. Studentenzimmer / Students' rooms

4. Gemeinschaftsraum / Communal room
5. Balkon / Balcony
6. Telefon / Telephone
7. Waschraum / Laundry room
8. Toiletten / Restrooms
9. Außentreppe / External staircase

Ansicht von Westen /
View from the west

1. Studenten-
restaurant /
Students'
restaurant
2. Eingangsterrasse /
Entrance terrace
3. Dienstleistungs-
zentrum für
Studenten /
Communal
students' services
center
4. Café / Café
5. Fußgänger-
arkade /
Pedestrian arcade

Empfang im Erdgeschoß / Reception on the ground floor

Fußgängerarkade / Pedestrian arcade

Treppenzugang kleine Wohneinheiten /
Entrance stairs to the small living units

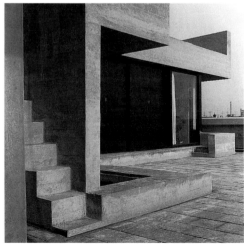

30

Wohnstraße für
Studentenehepaare /
Living street for
student couples

Sandkasten / Sandbox

Terrasse / Terrace

Innenansichten
Gemeinschaftsraum /
Interior views of
communal area

Studentenrestaurant im Keller- und Erdgeschoß /
Student restaurant on basement and ground floor

Montessorischule Delft
Delft, 1960–1966, 1968, 1970, 1981

Delftse Montessori School
Delft, 1960–1966, 1968, 1970, 1981

Das Schulgebäude wurde 1960 entworfen und verschiedentlich erweitert. Seine Raumgestaltung macht es möglich, daß mehrere Aktivitäten ungestört nebeneinander ablaufen können. Die Klassenzimmer haben fast durchweg einen L-förmigen Grundriß und schaffen damit abgegrenzte Lern- und Spielbereiche für die Kinder. Sie stoßen an einen breiten Flur, der sich diagonal durch das ganze Gebäude zieht. Überdies wurden Außenbereiche und Eingänge bewußt so gestaltet, daß vielfältig nutzbare Räume entstanden. Insbesondere wurde alles getan, um die Schwelle zwischen Außenwelt und Schule möglichst niedrig zu halten. So ist der Sportplatz außerhalb der Schulstunden auch für die Kinder aus der Nachbarschaft zugänglich.

This school, designed in 1960 but extended several times, permits through its spatial articulation activities to take place simultaneously without disturbing each other. The classrooms, almost all with an L-form shape in order to create different zones for the children to play or study, are placed along a wide corridor which meanders diagonally through the building. Also, to the outside zone and the entrances much attention has been given, creating spaces which can be used in many ways. Every effort has been made to soften the threshold between the outside world and the school. The playground is not closed off, but can be used by the neighbourhood children after school hours.

Mehrstufiger Erweiterungsplan / Plan of the extension phases

1960
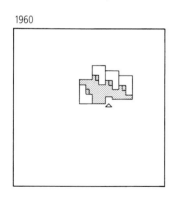

1966
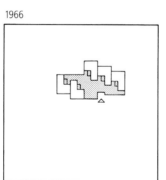

1968
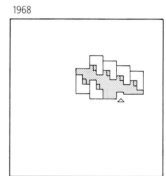

1970
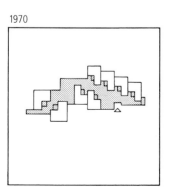

1981
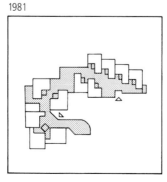

1999
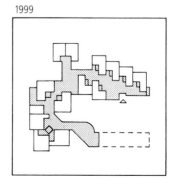

Haupteingang / Main entry

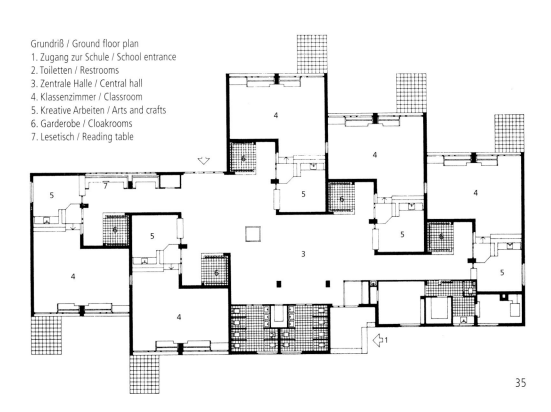

Grundriß / Ground floor plan
1. Zugang zur Schule / School entrance
2. Toiletten / Restrooms
3. Zentrale Halle / Central hall
4. Klassenzimmer / Classroom
5. Kreative Arbeiten / Arts and crafts
6. Garderobe / Cloakrooms
7. Lesetisch / Reading table

Halle mit Klassenzimmereingang / Hall with classroom entrance

Klassenzimmer / Classroom

Lesetisch / Reading table

Schnitt Eingang
Klassenzimmer /
Entrance classroom,
section

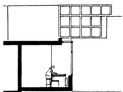

Sandkasten / Sandbox

Grundriß Klassenzimmer /
Classroom, ground plan

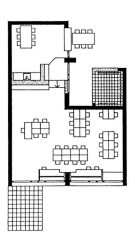

Erweiterung des Betriebsgebäudes LinMij
Amsterdam 1962–1964; 1995 abgerissen

Der Werkstattraum einer Großwäscherei wurde als erste Phase einer geplanten umfangreicheren Erweiterung auf dem Dach eines Gebäudes aus dem frühen zwanzigsten Jahrhundert errichtet. Man erwartete damals, daß sich in naher Zukunft neue Abteilungen entwickeln würden. Weitere Anbauten sollten folgen, so daß das alte Gebäude, dem jede Eigenart fehlte, schließlich von einem Geflecht baulicher Einheiten überwuchert wäre und die Gesamtanlage damit eine neue Identität erhielte. Der Architekt machte demonstrativen Gebrauch von Fertigbauteilen und Glas – beides in deutlichem Kontrast zum bestehenden alten Backsteinbau, dem Fundament für die neuen, leichteren Gebäudeteile. Wie der Architekt erklärte, garantierte das Material «die größtmögliche Sichtbarkeit – nicht nur der Außenwelt, sondern auch der Beschäftigten untereinander.» Gleichzeitig bot der Anbau mit seinen Fassaden aus Glas und Stein von außen her einen auffälligen Blickpunkt.

Extension to the Factory LinMij
Amsterdam, 1962–1964, demolished 1995

This workshop of a laundry factory was built on top of an early 20th century building. It was conceived as the first phase of extension. Other departments were expected to grow in the near future, leading to further extensions, so that in the end the old building, which had no particular character, would be overgrown by units capable of giving identity to the greater whole. The architect made demonstrative use of prefabricated parts and of glass. This in apparent contrast to the old brick building which forms the basis of the new light structures. This guaranteed, as the architect stated, a "maximum visiblity for those working there, not only of the world outside but more particularly of each other." At the same time, the extension with the glass and stone facades manifested itself as a spectacle from the outside.

Erweiterungsschema / Extension scheme

Aufgestocktes Gebäude / Raised building

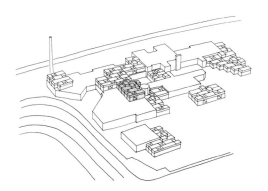

Teilansicht Fassade / Partial view facade

Innenfassade / Interior of the facade

1. Nähatelier /
   Sewing
   workshop
2. Loggia /
   Loggia

Schnitt und Grundriß / Section and ground plan

Kirche
Wettbewerb, Driebergen, 1964

Das spiralförmige Kirchengebäude ist ein architektonischer Raum mit halbdurchlässigem Charakter. Er basiert auf einem Raster von 1,5 x 1,5 Metern. Dem Architekten lag daran, einen Raum schaffen, der, wie er sagte, einerseits das Gespräch ermöglicht, es andererseits aber jedem freistellt, ob er sich am Gespräch beteiligen möchte; einen Raum, um zu sehen und gesehen zu werden, der aber auch die Möglichkeit läßt, sich abzusondern. Auf der Grundlage dieser Überlegungen entstand der Entwurf eines Gebäudes, das gleichzeitig formellen und informellem Charakter hat und sich darum nicht als einheitlicher, überblickbarer Raum präsentiert.

Church
Competition, Driebergen, 1964

The church, which has the form of a spiral, is an architectonic space with a diafragmatic character. It is based on a 1.5 by 1.5 meter module. The architect has chosen to create a space where, according to him, not only a dialogue should be possible, but also the possibility to choose to be a part of that dialogue or not. There should be room to see and to be seen, as well as space where one can find privacy. An attempt has been made to design a structure which works formally and informally at the same time. Therefore, there is not only one surveyable space.

Schnitte und Grundrisse / Sections and ground plans

Modell / Model

Perspektivische Skizze / Sketch in perspective

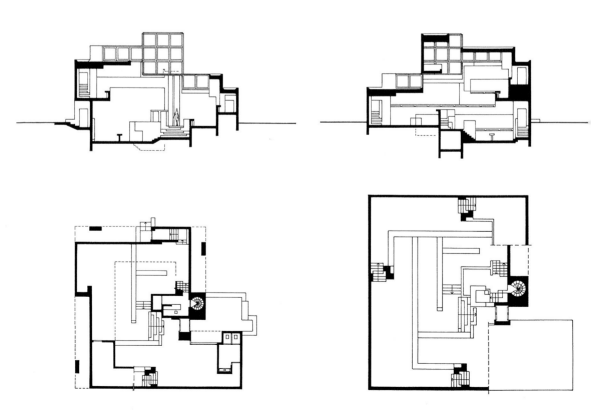

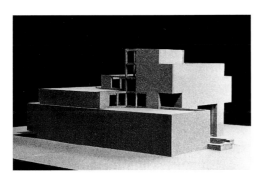

De Drie Hoven. Wohnanlage für Senioren und Behinderte
Amsterdam, 1964–1974

De Drie Hoven. Housing Complex for Elderly and Disabled People
Amsterdam, 1964–1974

Das Gebäude ist für körperlich und geistig behinderte Menschen bestimmt. Es umfaßt 55 Wohnungen für Ehepaare, Wohneinheiten für 190 Personen sowie ein Pflegeheim mit 250 Betten. Die besonderen Anforderungen der verschiedenen Abteilungen des Gebäudes sind im Rahmen einer umfassenden Gesamtstruktur berücksichtigt: einem System aus Stützen, Trägern und Decken, das innerhalb eines festen, konsistent angewandten Moduls eine große Freiheit der Raumnutzung erlaubt. Zugrunde liegt die Annahme, daß die ordnende Kraft dieser Grundstruktur ausreichen wird, um die Integration weiterer Ergänzungen, so unsystematisch sie auch ausfallen mögen, zu leisten, ohne dabei die Einheit ernsthaft zu gefährden. Auch in anderer Hinsicht ist das Gebäude als unvollendet zu bezeichnen: den verwendeten Materialien fehlen die Farben und «der letzte Schliff». So soll das unfertige Erscheinungsbild die Bewohner anregen, Interesse und Tatkraft zu entwickeln, um die Umgebung nach ihrem eigenen Gefallen zu gestalten.

The building, intended for physically and mentally challenged people, consists of 55 dwellings for couples, housing units for 190 people and a nursing home with 250 beds. The requirements for the different sections of the building are incorporated into a common building order; a system of columns, beams and floors, whereby, in a fixed and consistently applied module, a large amount of freedom in the utilisation of space arises. It is assumed that the regulating power of the basic structure will be great enough to enable the incorporation of subsequent additions, however chaotic, without its unity being severely disturbed. The structure can be regarded as incomplete in another respect as well, namely in the colourless and unfinished appearance of the materials used. It is hoped that this will stimulate the residents into exerting their influence in shaping the environment to their liking.

Hof im Nordwesten / Northwest court

Querschnitt / Cross section

Baugelände / Site

Vorgabeprogramm / Program

Raster mit theoretisch möglichen Türmen / Grid with theoretically possible towers

Überlagerung / Superimposition

Endgültiges Schema / Final scheme

Grundriß 2. Obergeschoß / Ground plan 2nd floor
1. Zentrale Halle: «Dorfplatz» /
   Central hall: "village green"
2. Betreuungstrakt / Care and welfare building
3. Pflegestation / Nursing ward
4. Haus mit Wohnungen für Ehepaare / Dwellings for couples
5. Personalhaus / Staff building

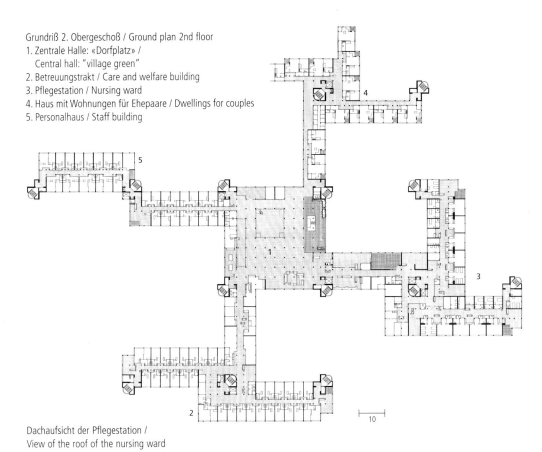

Dachaufsicht der Pflegestation /
View of the roof of the nursing ward

43

Garten / Garden

Terrasse / Terrace

Zentraler Gemeinschaftsraum / Central communal space

Wohnhäuser Diagoon
Delft, 1969–1970

Diagoon Housing
Delft, 1969–1970

Bestimmend für den Entwurf der acht experimentellen Wohnhäuser (Skeletthäuser) war die Vorstellung der prinzipiellen Unfertigkeit. Der Grundriß bleibt weitgehend offen, so daß die Bewohner selbst bestimmen können, wie sie den Raum einteilen und darin leben wollen, wo sie schlafen, wo sie essen und wo sie gemeinsam den Tag verbringen wollen. Wenn die Zusammensetzung einer Familie sich ändert, kann das Haus den veränderten Bedürfnissen angepaßt und innerhalb eines bestimmten Rahmens vergrößert werden. Der vorliegende Entwurf soll als Grundmodell betrachtet werden, das zahlreiche Variationen zuläßt. Die Freiheit, die den Bewohnern zur Einteilung und Vervollständigung ihres Hauses offensteht, könnte zu äußerst verschiedenartigen Raumgestaltungen führen. Die räumliche Anordnung schafft zahlreiche diagonale Blickachsen. Die Häuser sind als Prototypen entworfen, die in größerem Maßstab Verwendung finden können.

The main idea determining these 8 experimental houses (skeleton houses) is that they are in principle incomplete. The plan is indefinite so that the occupants themselves will be able to decide how to divide the space and live in it; where they will sleep, where they will eat, and where they will gather. If the composition of the family changes, the house can be adjusted and, to a certain extent, enlarged. What has been designed should be seen as an incomplete framework allowing a great number of variations. The freedom the inhabitants have to organize and finish their house could lead to the greatest possible diversity of spatial qualities. The spatial disposition permitted many diagonal views. The houses were conceived as prototypes which could be used on a larger scale.

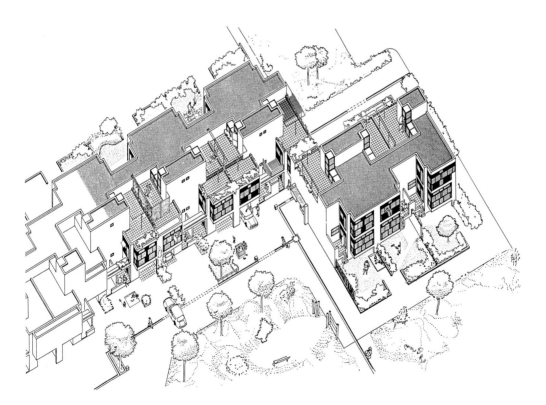

Grundidee des Hauses: Das Haus besteht aus zwei festen Kernen mit Geschoßebenen, die im Splitlevel versetzt sind. Diese Ebenen bilden die ‹Wohneinheiten› und können verschiedene Bestimmungen wie Wohn-, oder Schlafraum, Studier-, Spiel-, Sitz- oder Eßzimmer erhalten.

Basic idea of the house: The house consists of two fixed cores with half story high levels constituting the living units. These can accommodate a variety of functions: living, sleeping, studying, playing, dining.

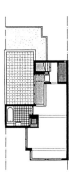

Querschnitt / Cross section

Grundrisse / Ground floor plans

Zentrales Atrium / Central atrium

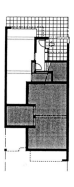

Siedlungsplan mit Diagoonhäusern als Prototypen /
Urban plan, with the Diagoon houses as prototypes

Gesamtansicht / General view

Fassade mit variablen Fensterrahmen /
Facade with variable window frames

Rathäuser
Wettbewerbe, Valkenswaard, 1966 und Amsterdam, 1967

Beide Projekte zeigen den strukturalistischen Ansatz, der im Bürogebäude Centraal Beheer seine volle Ausprägung erreicht. Das Rathaus von Valkenswaard bestand aus einem Ensemble durch Lufträume getrennter zwei- und dreigeschossiger Türme: der Gitterraster dieser Türme wurde zum Ausgangspunkt des Entwurfs. Bei der Planung des Amsterdamer Rathauses suchte man einen engeren Anschluß an den städtischen Kontext und situierte das Zentrum des Gebäudes mit den verschiedenen Ratssälen an der Kreuzung zweier Wegdiagonalen, die es in das Straßennetz der Umgebung einbinden. Der Architekt war der Ansicht, ein Rathaus müsse «der Gegenpol zu allem Monumentalen sein. Das Gebäude sollte sich nicht von seiner Umgebung absetzen, sondern so weit wie nur möglich in den städtischen Raum integriert sein.»

Town Halls
Competitions, Valkenswaard, 1966 and Amsterdam, 1967

Both projects were determined by a structuralist approach which culminated in the Centraal Beheer office building. The Town Hall of Valkenswaard consisted of towers of two or three storeys with voids between them. The grid of the towers was the point of departure for the plan. In the design for the Town Hall of Amsterdam, the plan had a stronger connection with the urban fabric, and the heart of the building with the various council halls was placed at the intersection of two diagonal paths which linked it to the surrounding streets. The architect was of the opinion that a "town hall must be essentially anti-monumental. The building should not try to stand apart from the surrounding city, but fit in as much as possible in the environment."

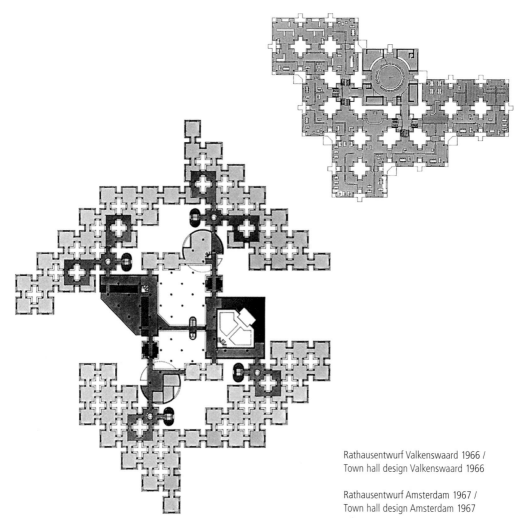

Rathausentwurf Valkenswaard 1966 /
Town hall design Valkenswaard 1966

Rathausentwurf Amsterdam 1967 /
Town hall design Amsterdam 1967

Zum Vergleich: Centraal Beheer 1968–1972 /
For comparison: Centraal Beheer 1968–1972

Centraal Beheer. Bürogebäude
Apeldoorn, 1968–1972

Diese «Werkstatt für tausend Menschen» ist ein bahn-brechendes Oeuvre, die Krönung von Hertzbergers struk-turalistischer Bauweise. Das Raumsystem des Gebäudes beruht wie in den zwei Rathausprojekten auf einem drei-dimensionalen Gitterraster und setzt sich aus Gruppen quadratischer «Büro-Inseln» zusammen, zwischen denen offene Lufträume das Gebäude in voller Höhe durch-stoßen. Eine Vielfalt von Durchgängen erschließt den Ge-samtraum und gewährt ein Maximum visueller Verbin-dungen. Organisatorische Veränderungen, die im Lauf der Zeit nötig wurden, ließen sich ausnahmslos innerhalb des ursprünglichen Gebäuderahmens durchführen. Bemer-kenswerterweise besaß eine Versicherungsgesellschaft den Weitblick und den Geschäftssinn, die einer Kommu-ne fehlten. (Erweiterung 1990–1995, siehe S. 134 ff.)

Centraal Beheer. Office Building
Apeldoorn, 1968–1972

This "workshop for a thousand people" is a pathbreaking work and marks the summit of his structuralist architec-ture. As in the two projects for town halls the diagram of this office building was based on a three-dimensional grid. The diagram consists of clusters of square office "is-lands" separated by top-lit voids that penetrate all levels. A large variety of passageways form the circulation routes and provide a maximum of visual connections. The build-ing proved capable of accommodating all of the organi-sational adjustments which were demanded in the course of time. Striking enough, the insurance company had the vision and business acumen that the government lacked. (Extension 1990–1995, see pp. 134–137)

Personalrestaurant / Restaurant for employees

Situationsplan / Site plan

Luftansicht / Aerial view

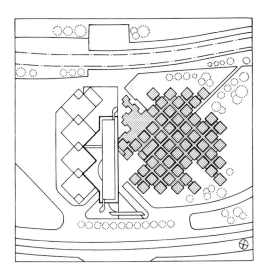 

Zentrales Atrium mit Innenteich / Central atrium with pond

Perspektivischer Schnitt / Section in perspective

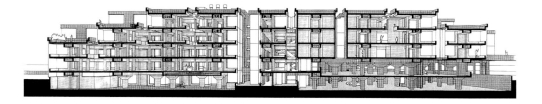

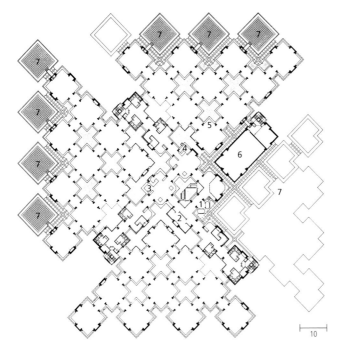

Grundriß 4. Stock / Ground plan 4th floor
1. Fahrstuhl / Elevator
2. Garderobe / Cloakroom
3. Café / Café
4. Empfang / Reception
5. Büroraum / Office space
6. Technischer Turm / Technical tower
7. Dachterrassen / Roof terraces

Teilansicht mit Parkhaus /
Partial view with parking garage

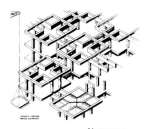

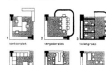

primaire bouwstenen

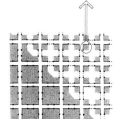

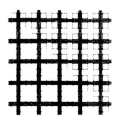

Blick auf den Zentralbereich /
View of the central area

Darstellung der primären Bauteile /
Scheme of the primary building components

Übersicht über die Büroeinheiten /
View of the office units

Musikzentrum Vredenburg
Utrecht, 1973–1978

Vredenburg Music Center
Utrecht, 1973–1978

Das auf einem Marktplatz gelegene Gebäude gibt sich nicht als exquisiter «Tempel der Musik», sondern will von der Stadt absorbiert werden. Das Gebäude enthält außer dem Musikzentrum auch Geschäfte, Büros, Cafés und ein Informationszentrum. Das Musikzentrum ist von der umlaufenden Ladenarkade her zugänglich, die sich an ein bestehendes Einkaufszentrum anschließt. Von den Foyers fällt der Blick in die Arkade. Sowohl der Hauptkonzertsaal wie der mit einer separaten Glaskuppel gedeckte, kleinere Saal sind so entworfen, daß sie mehrfach genutzt werden können. «Ein Gebäude ist in erster Linie dazu da, Funktionen zu erfüllen,» hielt der Architekt einmal fest, «doch nicht nur als passive und sozusagen willfährige Organisationsmaschine, die einen reibungslosen Ablauf garantiert. Es muß, soweit möglich, auch aktiv zum emotionalen Erleben der Benutzer beitragen. (...) Damit ist nicht nur gemeint, daß Erlebnisinhalte geboten werden müssen – der Raum und die Mittel seiner Gestaltung sollten außerdem als deren Resonanzboden dienen.»

Rather than trying to distinguish itself as a "temple of music", the building, situated on a market square, seeks to be absorbed by the city. The building comprises not only the music center but also shops, offices, cafes, and an information center. The music center is accessible from the surrounding shopping arcade, which is a continuation of an existent shopping center. From the foyers, one has a view of the arcade. The main concert hall, like the small concert hall with its own glass dome, is designed to accommodate a variety of uses. As the architect once stated: "Above all a building must function, but not only as a passive and, as it were, quiescent organisation, so that everything runs smoothly. It must also, where possible, make an active contribution to the emotional experience of the users (...). Not only should there be something to experience in itself, but the space and the means by which it is shaped must also act as a sounding-board for it."

Großer Saal / Large auditorium

Ansicht Eingangsfassade /
View of the entrance facade

Ansicht Westfassade /
View of the west facade

Großer Saal / Large auditorium

«Informelle Bänke» im großen Saal / "Informal benches" in the large auditorium

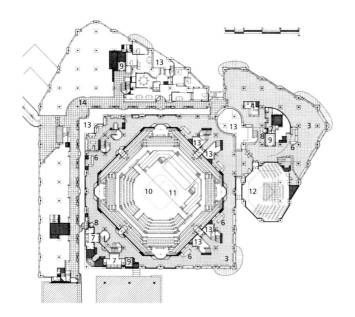

Grundriß 1. Obergeschoß /
1st floor plan

Grundriß Erdgeschoß /
Ground floor plan

1. Kartenverkauf / Ticket office
2. Haupteingang großer Saal /
   Main entrance large auditorium
3. Foyer / Foyer
4. Garderobe, bewacht /
   Cloakroom, attended
5. Garderobe, unbewacht /
   Cloakroom, unattended
6. Buffet / Buffet
7. Toiletten / Restrooms
8. Telefon / Telephone
9. Aufzug / Elevator
10. Großer Saal, 1700 Sitzplätze /
    Large auditorium, 1700 seats
11. Podium
12. Kleiner Saal, 250 Sitzplätze /
    Small auditorium, 250 seats
13. Luftraum / Air space
14. Öffentliche Passage /
    Public passage way
15. Information / Information

Schnitt / Section

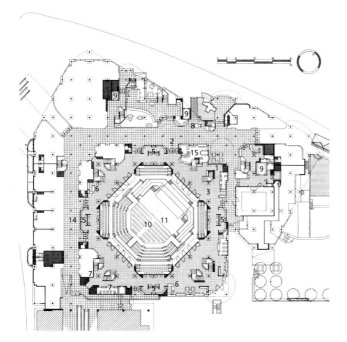

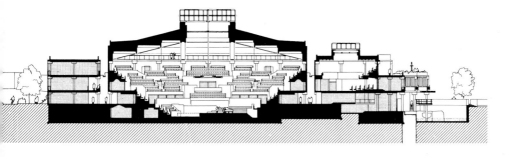

Foyer vor dem kleinen Saal /
Foyer to small auditorium

Passage way / Arcade

Entwurfsskizze /
Design sketch

Haarlemmer Houttuinen. Wohnungsbauprojekt
Amsterdam, 1979–1982

Das Hauptthema des Projekts ist die «Wohnstraße», die in Zusammenarbeit mit den Architekten Van Herk und Nagelkerke, den Leitern des Projekts auf der gegenüberliegenden Straßenseite, entwickelt wurde. Die Straße ist eine verkehrsfreie Quartierstraße. Durch die weit vorspringenden Balkone auf Stützpfeilern erhält die Straße einen besonderen Rhythmus. Der Architekt schrieb dazu: «Vorausgesetzt, wir bemühen uns in unserem Entwurf um die richtige Raumdisposition, so werden die Bewohnerinnen und Bewohner eher dazu geneigt sein, ihre Einflußsphäre bis in den öffentlichen Raum hinein auszudehnen. Das bedeutet, daß auf den Außenraum, der damit der persönlichen Zuwendung unterliegt, weit mehr Liebe verwandt wird, als man dem öffentlichen Raum üblicherweise zukommen läßt. Seine Qualität dürfte sich in der Folge gewaltig verbessern, was besonders im Interesse der Allgemeinheit liegt.»

Haarlemmer Houttuinen. Housing
Amsterdam, 1979–1982

The main theme of the project is the "living street", which was elaborated in collaboration with Van Herk and Nagelkerke, the architects leading the project across the street. This street is an access road and is not accessable to traffic. The long housing block has projecting piers with balconies that give a special rhythm to the street. The architect wrote: "Provided we make the effort to incorporate the proper spatial suggestions in our design, the inhabitants will be more inclined to expand their sphere of influence outwardly to the public area. Much more love is lavished on this exterior space, which has thus come under personal care, than is usual in the case of public spaces, and the quality will thus be fantastically increased notably in the common interest".

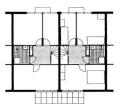

Eingangsbereich zu vier Wohnungen /
Entry zone to four apartments

Grundrisse / Ground plans

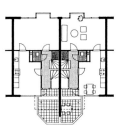

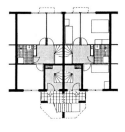

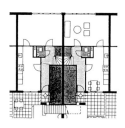

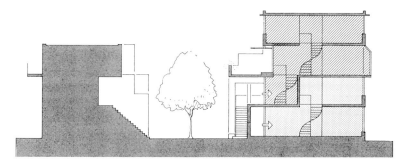

Schnitt / Section

Wohnstraße / Living street

Wohnungsbau
Kassel, Deutschland, 1979–1982

«In einem Mehrfamilienhaus sollten nicht ausschließlich die architektonischen Maßnahmen zur Verhinderung exzessiver Lärmbelästigung und anderer Störungen durch die Nachbarn im Mittelpunkt stehen. Aufmerksamkeit verdient insbesondere die Raumgestaltung, denn sie beeinflußt die zu erwartenden sozialen Kontakte zwischen den Hausbewohnern. Aus diesem Grund besitzt das Treppenhaus eine größere Bedeutung als üblich.» Die Treppen, die als «vertikale Straßen» konzipiert sind, führen auf Dachterrassen und bieten auf einem halbkreisförmigen Treppenabsatz einen Gemeinschaftsspielplatz. Der Übergang von den Wohnungen zum Treppenhaus ist als Zwischenzone gestaltet: eine durchsichtige Tür führt zur Treppe, eine feste Tür in den Wohnbereich.

Housing
Kassel, Germany, 1979–1982

"In a multi-family house the emphasis should not lie exclusively on the architectural provisions to prevent excess noise and inconvenience from neighbours; special attention must be paid in particular to the spatial disposition which is conducive to the social contacts expected to exist between the occupants of a building. Therefore, we have given the staircases more prominence than usual". The staircases, designed as "vertical streets" leading to roof terraces, have a semi-circular landing which provides a communal playground. From the dwellings, the transition to the staircase is made by an in between zone, with a transparent door towards the stairs and a solid one towards the dwelling unit.

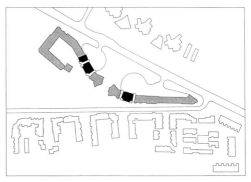

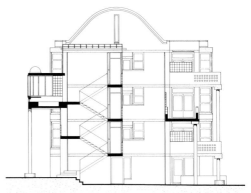

Treppenhaus als «vertikale Straße»/
Staircase as "vertical street"

Situationsschema /
Site scheme

Schnitt Treppenhaus /
Section staircase

Ansicht Balkonseite /
View balcony side

Grundriß / Ground plan

Alternativer Balkontyp /
Alternative balcony type

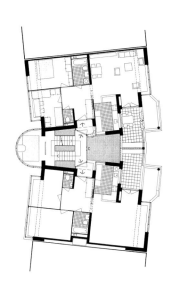

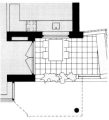

Ministerium für Arbeit und
Soziale Angelegenheiten
Den Haag, 1979–1990

Ministry of Social Welfare
and Employment
The Hague, 1979–1990

1980 hatte Hertzberger den ersten, vorläufigen Entwurf für ein neues Ministeriumsgebäude vorgelegt, das auf einem Grundstück parallel zu den Gleisanlagen entstehen sollte. 1985 erhielt er den Auftrag für einen definitiven Projektentwurf. Das Gebäude hat ein normales Skelett, bei dessen Bau eine große Zahl von Elementen wiederholte Verwendung fand. Diese Anlage erlaubte nicht nur eine Rationalisierung, sondern ließ auch Freiheit bei der Ausführung des Bauprogramms. Anstelle eines Bauvolumens mit weitläufigen Büroflächen wählte der Architekt die Form verschiedener Einheiten, die ein langgezogenes räumliches Zentrum umgeben. Auf der einen Seite sind die einzelnen Einheiten so hoch, daß man von den Büroräumen das Eisenbahngelände überblickt. Auf der anderen Seite sind sie in Übereinstimmung mit der Höhe der Nachbargebäude so niedrig wie möglich gehalten.

After having submitted in 1980 the first provisional design for a new ministry building located on a site parallel to the railway tracks, Hertzberger was asked in 1985 to make a definitive scheme for this project. The building has a regular skeleton, built with a repetition of a large amount of elements. The configuration not only allowed a rationalisation but also a freedom in accommodating the building program. Instead of an architectural volume containing vast office spaces, the architect opted for an articulation into different building units placed along an elongated central space. On one side the building units rise so that from the office spaces there is a view over the train embankment. On the other side they have been kept as low as possible, conforming to the height of the housing in the area.

Zentrales Atrium mit Café / Central atrium with café

Übersicht über alle Stützen- und Trägerschnittpunkte / Survey of all column and beam connections

Beispiel für einen Stützen- und Trägerschnittpunkt / Example of a column and beam connection

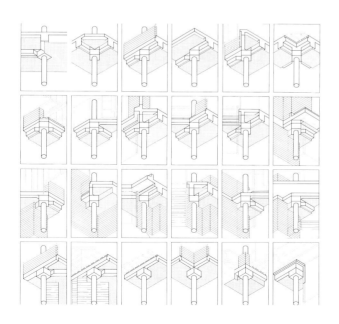

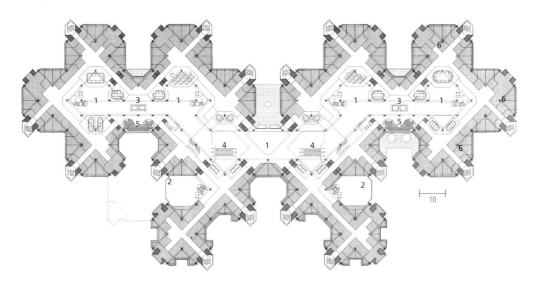

Grundriß 2. Obergeschoß /
2nd floor plan

Schema Atrium / Atrium scheme

Luftansicht von Norden /
Aerial view from the north

Haupteingang / Main entrance

1. Zentrales Atrium /
   Central atrium
2. Nebenatrium /
   Smaller atrium
3. Aufzüge / Elevators
4. Rolltreppe / Escalators
5. Toiletten / Restrooms
6. Büroräume / Office spaces

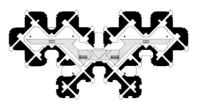

Zentrale Durchgangspassage /
Central passage way

Treppenhaus in der zentralen Passage /
staircase in the central passage way

Detail Beleuchtung / detail lighting fixture

Apolloschulen
Amsterdam, 1980–1983

Apollo Schools
Amsterdam, 1980–1983

Die beiden Schulgebäude sind aus demselben Programm hervorgegangen und weisen nicht zuletzt aus diesem Grund in ihrer strukturellen Grammatik und Gesamtanlage zahlreiche Gemeinsamkeiten auf. Die dennoch bestehenden Unterschiede haben nicht nur in unterschiedlichen schulpädagogischen Auffassungen ihren Grund, sondern auch in der unterschiedlichen Lage der Bauten auf dem Grundstück und der daraus folgenden unterschiedlichen Orientierung der Erkerfenster. Der beschränkte Baugrund und die Umgebung zwangen zur Konzentration auf kompakte Volumen (sozusagen städtische Villen), die sich durch große Transparenz und strukturelle Klarheit auszeichnen. Die Klassenzimmer sind um ein zentrales Foyer angeordnet, das zusammen mit den Treppen wie ein Amphitheater wirkt. In die großzügig angelegte Treppe außerhalb des Hauses, die in die Spiele auf dem Schulhof einbezogen werden kann, ist der Eingang zu den Räumen des Kindergartens integriert.

In their structural grammar and general disposition the two schools show many similarities between them, mainly because they originated from the same program. The differences are not only the result of different school philosophies but also of their different positions on the site and the, consequently, different orientation of the bay windows. The restricted building site and the surroundings led to compact buildings (urban villas in a way) which show a great transparency and structural clarity on the inside. The classrooms are grouped around a central hall which, together with the stairs, has the quality of an amphitheater. On the outside, the generously proportioned staircases, which function as play elements on the school square, also give shelter to the entrance of the kindergarten rooms.

Montessorischule (links), Willemsparkschule (rechts) /
Montessori school (left), Willemspark school (right)

Eingang Spielplatz / Entrance to playground

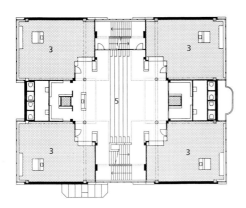

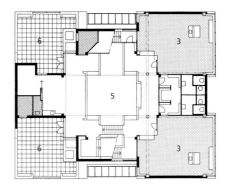

Grundrisse und Schnitte / Floor plans and sections
1. Eingang / Entrance
2. Halle Kindergarten / Hall kindergarten
3. Klassenzimmer / Classroom
4. Spielraum / Playroom
5. Zentrale Halle / Central hall
6. Terrasse / Terrace

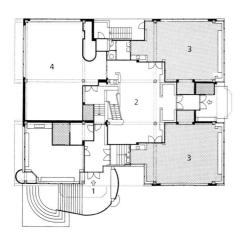

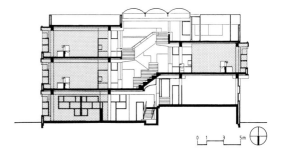

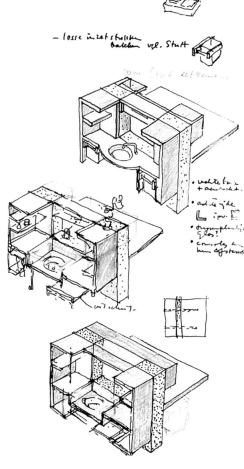

Küchenelement für Klassen
der Unterstufe und Kindergarten /
Kitchen block for the lower
grades and the kindergarten

Entwurfsskizze Küchenelement /
Design sketch kitchen block

Arbeiten in der Halle /
Working in the hall

Innenansichten der Halle /
Interiour views of the hall

81

Zentrale Halle mit Sitzstufen / Central hall with steps

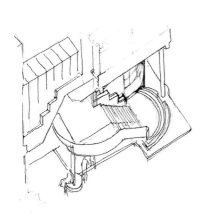 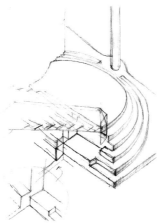

Eingangsseite
Willemsparkschule /
Willemspark school,
entrance side

Skizze / Sketch

Eingangstreppe
Willemsparkschule /
Willemspark school,
entrance staircase

De Overloop. Seniorenwohnanlage
Almere Haven, 1980–1984

Das Altenheim liegt am Deich, der Grenze zwischen Land und Meer, und läßt den Blick auf den See frei. Für das Gebäude stand der beschränkte Raum einer Baulücke zwischen einer Parkgarage, einer Schule und einer zum Deich führenden Straße zur Verfügung. Die Anlage umschließt einen Hof, der den Bewohner, die nur kurze Spaziergänge unternehmen können, die Annehmlichkeiten eines windgeschützten «Miniaturparks» bietet. Die Halle im Mittelpunkt des Gebäudes ist das lebendige Zentrum des Heims. Sie ist durch alle Stockwerke nach oben geöffnet und fungiert als natürlicher Konvergenzpunkt für die Bewohner. Während das Hauptgebäude 84 Einer- und 8 Zweierapartments enthält, stehen den noch unabhängiger lebenden Heimbewohnern im niedrigeren, U-förmigen Ostflügel 18 Wohneinheiten für zwei Personen zur Verfügung.

De Overloop. Housing for the Elderly
Almere Haven, 1980–1984

Situated overlooking the lake, along the dike marking the boundary between land and water, the building had to be inserted into the cramped space left between a parking-garage, a school and a road leading to the dike. The complex surrounds and protects from the winds a courtyard which offers to those unable to undertake more than brief strolls the pleasures of a "miniature" park. The central hall is the heart of the building. It extends vertically across all storeys and acts as a natural point of convergence for the residents. Whereas the main building has 84 single-person and 8 two-persons apartments, the less high U-shaped wing on the east side consists of 18 two-person units for those who are more independent.

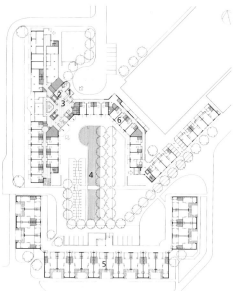

Situation / Site plan
1. Haupteingang / Main entrance
2. Empfang / Reception area
3. Halle / Lobby
4. Garten / Garden
5. Wohnungen für Ehepaare /
   Apartments for couples
6. Betreuungstrakt /
   Care and welfare building

Schnitt / Section

Ansicht Innenhof / View of courtyard

Gemeinschaftsraum / Communal space

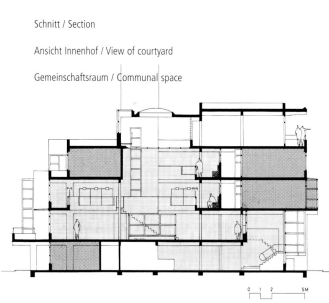

0 1 2   5M

LiMa. Wohnungsbau
Berlin, 1982–1986

Die Lage des Grundstücks erforderte den Anschluß an einen bestehenden Wohnblock. Zu berücksichtigen war außerdem die unmittelbare Nähe einer Kirche, die eine einfache Lösung unmöglich machte. Die schließlich gewählte halbrunde Anlage läßt den Standort der Kirche als unabhängiges, freistehendes Bauwerk unbeeinträchtigt. Der Grundriß zeigt, daß eine gute Hofrandbebauung dann möglich ist, wenn die Wohnungen genug Sonne erhalten und die Proportionen des Innenhofs die Anlage eines Gartens und Kinderspielplatzes erlauben. Von der Straße her ist der Hof durch fünf Tore erschlossen. Sie sind Teil der Treppenzonen, die zu den Wohnungen und Terrassen führen, und als vertikale Straßen gedacht, die zu Begegnungen einladen. Unter dem Innenhof liegt eine Parkgarage.

LiMa. Residential Building
Berlin, Germany, 1982–1986

The site demanded the completion of an existing building block. The presence of a church made a straightforward solution impossible. Therefore, a semi-circular solution was found which left the church standing as an independent, free-standing structure. The plan shows that it is possible to build good housing around a courtyard, when enough sunshine can be ensured and when the courtyard is thus proportioned that there is sufficient space for a garden area and for children to play. Five gateways make the courtyard accessible from the street. These entrances form part of the communal staircase realms, which lead to the apartments and terraces and which have been conceived as vertical streets where people can meet. Underneath the courtyard is a parking garage.

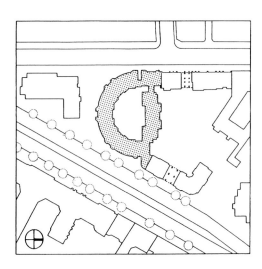

Situationsschema / Site scheme

Axonometrie / Axonometric view

Entwurfsskizze / Design sketch

Wohnungstypen / Apartment types

Teilansicht / Partial view

Balkon / Balcony

Wohnzimmer / Living room

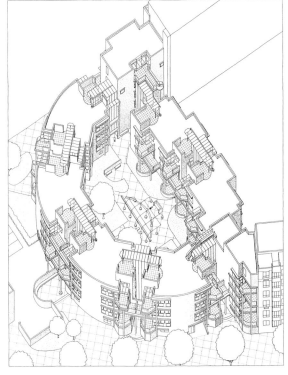

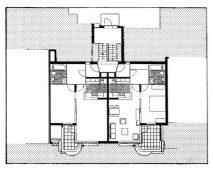

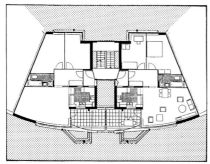

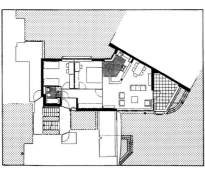

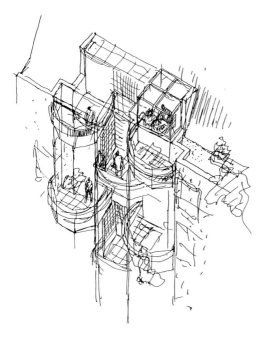

De Evenaar. Schule und Kindergarten
Amsterdam, 1984–1986

Die Anordnung der Klassenzimmer, die um ein Foyer im Mittelpunkt des Gebäudes gruppiert sind, ist eine Weiterentwicklung des Bauprinzips der Amsterdamer Apolloschulen. Hier sind auf jedem Stockwerk aber nicht mehr zwei, sondern drei Klassenräume mit versetzten Geschossen zusammengefaßt und spiralförmig um das zentrale Foyer angeordnet. Anders als in den Apolloschulen, wo Kindergarten und Grundschule getrennt sind, galt hier eine möglichst weitgehende räumliche Integration verschiedener Altersgruppen als erwünschtes pädagogisches Ziel. Wenn sich die Notwendigkeit ergibt, kann der Bereich für die Jüngsten allerdings durch eine Schiebetüre vom Foyer getrennt werden. Die Glaswände der Klassenzimmer sind als geschwungene Fensterfront entworfen: Je zwei Klassenzimmer bilden ein räumliches «Bogenfenster», was besonders dann sichtbar wird, wenn die Faltwände zwischen den Klassen geöffnet sind. Die Halle mit den Stufen eines Amphitheaters und dem großen Dachflächenfenster kann für Treffen verschiedenster Art genutzt werden. Die Schule liegt leicht zugänglich an einem öffentlichen Platz, und die Treppe zum Haupteingang mit ihren Tribünensitzen spielt im sozialen Leben des Platzes eine wichtige Rolle.

De Evenaar. Kindergarten and School
Amsterdam, 1984–1986

The lay-out of the classrooms, which are grouped around the central hall, further develops the principle of the Apollo Schools in Amsterdam. Here, however, the classrooms are not grouped in two, but three per floor. The groups of classrooms in split level on opposite sides are arranged spiral-wise around the central hall. Unlike the Apollo Schools, where the kindergarten is shielded from the primary school, here the most complete as possible spatial integration of the different age groups fulfils the desired educational goals. Nevertheless, whenever necessary, the area of the youngest children can be divided from the central hall by a sliding door. The glass walls of the classrooms are designed as bay windows in such a way that two classes compose one spatial "bow" window, especially when the sliding partition between them is open. The central hall with its amphitheater steps and big skylight can be used for gatherings of various purposes. The school is freely situated on a public square. The main stairway with its tribunal seats plays an important role on this square.

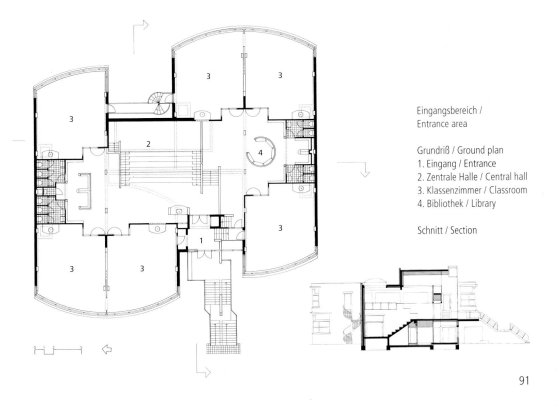

Eingangsbereich /
Entrance area

Grundriß / Ground plan
1. Eingang / Entrance
2. Zentrale Halle / Central hall
3. Klassenzimmer / Classroom
4. Bibliothek / Library

Schnitt / Section

Schulhof /
Schoolyard

Küchenelement /
Kitchen block

Zentrale Halle /
Central hall

Innenansicht
Klassenzimmer /
Interior view
of the classroom

Filmzentrum Esplanade
Wettbewerb, Berlin, 1986

Esplanade Film Center
Competition, Berlin, Germany, 1986

Das Projekt, dessen Entwurfsgeschichte mehrere Phasen umfaßt, enthält eine Akademie, ein Museum, eine Bibliothek, einen zentral gelegenen Versorgungsbereich, Verwaltungsräumlichkeiten und einen Empfangsbereich mit Restaurant. Für die verschiedenen Funktionen sind voneinander unabhängige Gebäude vorgesehen, die zusammen einen Komplex bilden, der durch die einheitliche Formensprache als Ganzes kenntlich wird. Im Zentrum des Komplexes liegen das Gebäude des alten Kinos Esplanade und ein Platz, den Satelliten säumen, die durch Übergänge und Arkaden verbunden sind.

Interessanterweise wurde im ersten Entwurf des Architekten eine Verbindung zum bestehenden Kulturforum geschaffen, wodurch die Grundstücksgrenzen überschritten wurde.

This project, of which the design history shows more stages, contains an academy, a museum, a library, a central service area, administration spaces and a reception area with a restaurant. All these functions are located in independent buildings that together make up a conglomerate recognisable as a whole by the use of the same design language. At the center of the complex are the old Esplanade building and a piazza, around which satellites have been placed. These discs are connected by elevated walkways and arcades.

Interesting is that, in the first design the architect made a connection with the existing Kulturforum, thus going over the site boundaries.

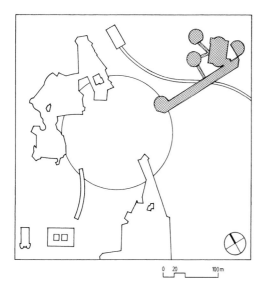

0   20   100 m

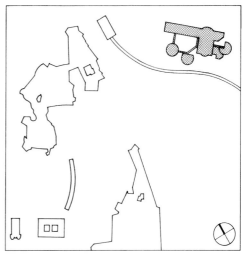

Wettbewerbsentwurf / Competition design

Zweiter Entwurf / Second design

Ursprüngliche Vorderfront des Hotels Esplanade /
Original facade of the Esplanade Hotel

Ansichtszeichnung / View, drawing

Entwurfsskizze / Design sketch

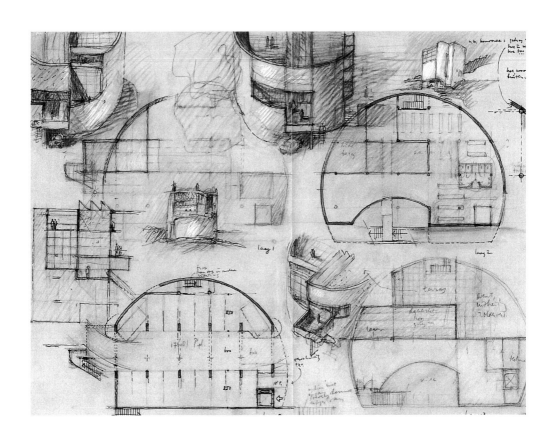

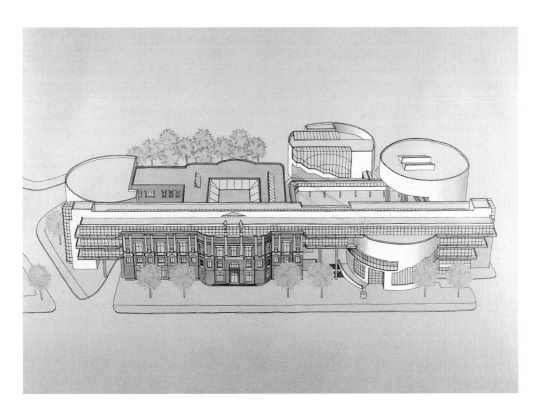

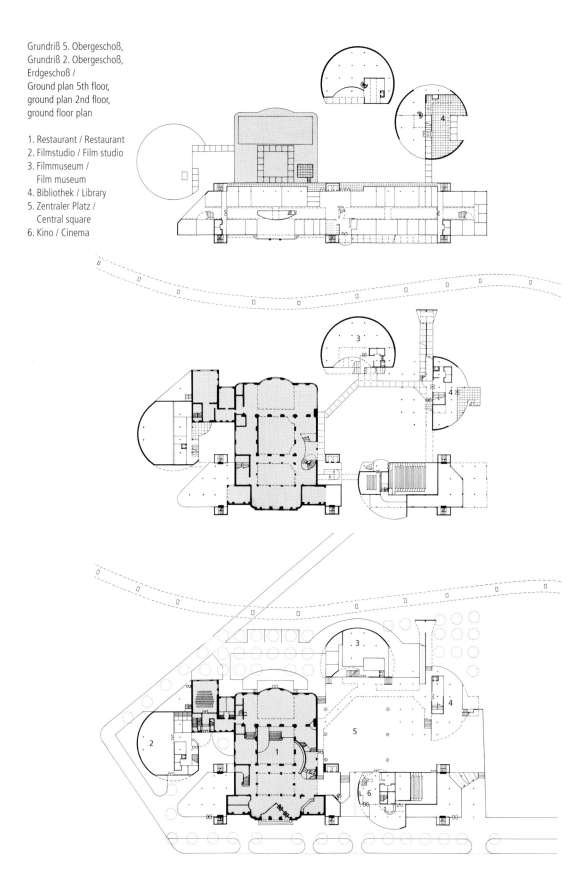

Grundriß 5. Obergeschoß,
Grundriß 2. Obergeschoß,
Erdgeschoß /
Ground plan 5th floor,
ground plan 2nd floor,
ground floor plan

1. Restaurant / Restaurant
2. Filmstudio / Film studio
3. Filmmuseum /
   Film museum
4. Bibliothek / Library
5. Zentraler Platz /
   Central square
6. Kino / Cinema

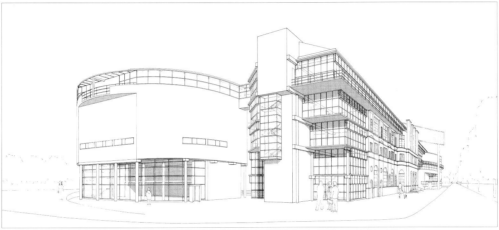

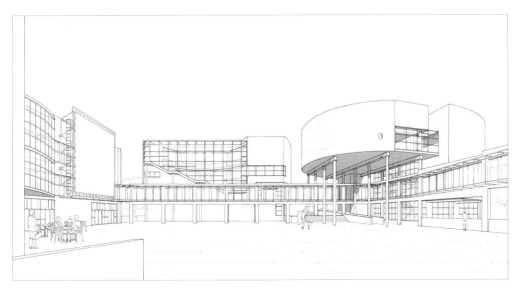

Südwestansicht, Ansicht vom Platz, Südostansicht /
View from the southwest, from the square and from the southeast

Theaterzentrum Spui
Den Haag, 1986–1993

Spui Theater Center
The Hague, 1986–1993

Der Komplex liegt im Herzen Den Haags und bildet ein wichtiges Element der Konzentration von kulturellen Gebäuden in der neuen Innenstadt, zu denen unter anderem das «Muziek- und Danstheater» und das neue Rathaus gehören. Das Zentrum beherbergt zwei Vortragssäle, ein Kino, ein Videozentrum, eine Kunstgalerie und ein Theater sowie Geschäfte und 76 Wohnungen. Der kompakte Gesamtkomplex bildet eine kleine Stadt für sich. Die Krümmung eines Wohnungsriegels legt nicht nur die Ausrichtung des Gebäudes fest, sondern ermöglicht darüber hinaus eine bessere Sicht auf die aus dem 17. Jahrhundert stammende Neue Kirche, die leicht zurückgesetzt neben dem neuen Ensemble liegt. Unter der Geschoßkurve stößt ein weitläufiges Foyer ins Gebäude vor und zieht die Straße sozusagen bis ins Zentrum der Anlage.

The complex is located in the center of The Hague and forms an important element in the new concentration of cultural buildings, such as the dance theater and the new town hall. The center houses two auditoriums, a movie theater, a video center, an art gallery and a theater, as well as shops and 76 dwellings. The whole compact complex is a little city in itself. The housing levels are partly curved, not only for giving the building a direction, but also to clear the way for a broader view of the 17th century New Church, which lies next to the building set behind the building line. Underneath the curve the building is penetrated by a large foyer that pulls the street, as it were, into the heart of the complex.

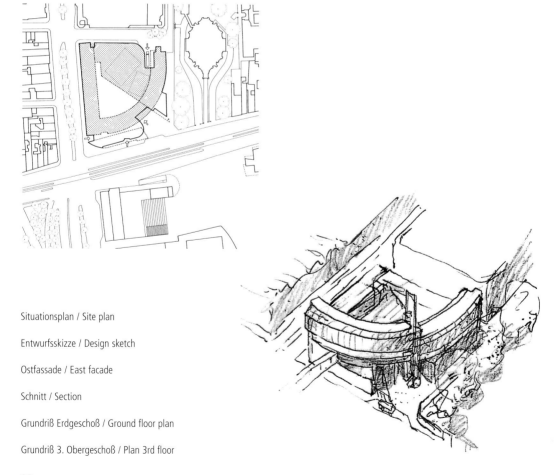

Situationsplan / Site plan

Entwurfsskizze / Design sketch

Ostfassade / East facade

Schnitt / Section

Grundriß Erdgeschoß / Ground floor plan

Grundriß 3. Obergeschoß / Plan 3rd floor

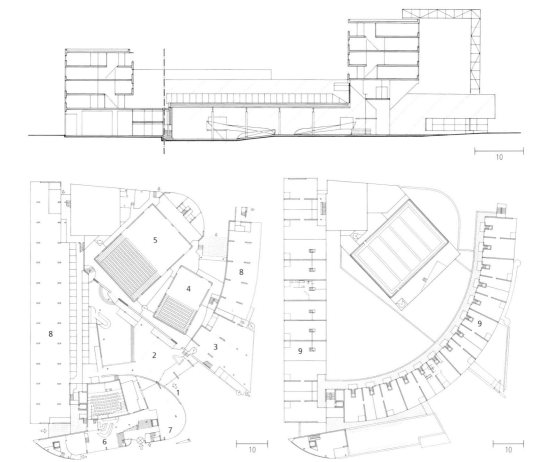

1. Eingang Theater / Entrance theater
2. Foyer / Foyer
3. Café / Café
4. Kleiner Saal / Small theater hall

5. Großer Saal / Large auditorium
6. Filmzentrum / Film center
7. Videozentrum / Video center
8. Geschäfte / Shops
9. Wohnungen / Apartments

Teilansicht der Westfassade / Partial view of the west facade

Laubengang zu den Wohnungen / Gallery leading to the apartments

Foyer / Foyer

Das Foyer wird wie ein Saal genutzt. / The foyer is used as an auditorium.

Häuser auf dem Wasser.
Experimentelle Wohnungen
Projekt, Haarlem, 1986

Die Vorstellung, auf dem Wasser zu leben, ist nichts Neues. Dennoch erscheint es sinnvoll, diesem Gedanken in den Niederlanden, einem Land des Wassers, neuen Ausdruck zu geben. Natürlich kennt jeder die Hausboote, die oft ein lebendiges Bild individuellen Erfindergeistes vermitteln. Aber sie sind vor allem Boote und erst in zweiter Linie Wohnraum, zumal dann, wenn sie in Längsrichtung am Kai vertäut sind. Die zylindrische Form der Häuser, mit einem Ausschnitt für die Terrassen, steht im Dienst einer möglichst kompakten Raumstruktur. Die Ausrichtung der Häuser kann je nach Wunsch der Bewohner durch Drehung verändert werden. Damit ändern sich auch Lichteinfall und Ausblick. Die Häuser müßten auf Betonflößen errichtet werden, die mit Isoliermaterial gefüllt sind.

Waterhouses.
Experimental Housing
Project, Haarlem, 1986

The thought of living on water is not new, but it does make sense to give form to this thought in a new way in a water country like the Netherlands. Of course we all know the houseboats which often express a lively image of individual inventiveness, but especially where they are put in a longitudinal manner along the quays they are first of all boat and only in second place habitation. The cylindrical form, of which a section has been cut out for the terrace, was used in order to arrive at the most compact possible organisation of the houses. The orientation of the house can be rotated according to the wishes of the inhabitants, and thus the light and view can be changed. The houses would have to be built on concrete floats filled with insulating material.

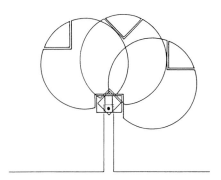 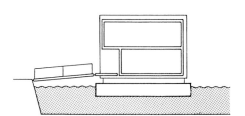

Die Häuser schwimmen auf Betonflößen. Um ihre Beweglichkeit zu sichern,
wurden die Versorgungs- und Abwasserleitungen mit dem Zugangssteg über lösliche Gelenke verbunden. /

The houses are floating on concrete waggons. They can be moved.
Consequently the installation conducts are assembled in a flexible way.

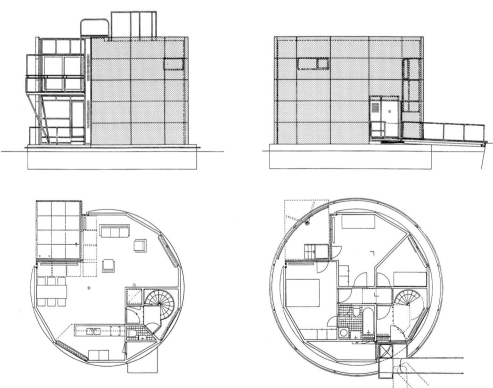

Modell / Model

Aufrisse / Elevations

Grundriß Erdgeschoß und 1. Obergeschoß / Ground floor and 1st floor plan

Bicocca. Projekt für Pirelli
Wettbewerb, Mailand, 1986

Bicocca. Project for Pirelli
Competition, Milan, Italy, 1986

Der Grundriß besteht im wesentlichen aus Gebäude-reihen, die die Proportionen des Straßennetzes und der bestehenden Bausubstanz aufnehmen. In Ergänzung der Gebäude, die erhalten bleiben sollen, können innerhalb dieser Struktur unterschiedliche Gebäudetypen, aber auch unterschiedliche Funktionen Raum finden. Die praktische Ausführung des Plans kann sich über eine längere Zeit-spanne erstrecken und vielfältigere Formen annehmen, als sich in einem Entwurf festhalten läßt. Der Gesamtent-wurf läßt sich also mit einem urbanen Strukturgeflecht vergleichen, das aus Kette und Schuß besteht. Wenn wir uns das Endresultat als Webgeflecht denken, repräsentiert unser Entwurf nur den Schuß. Als Kettfäden fungieren dann die verschiedenen Bedürfnisse, die sich aus der praktischen Nutzung ergeben. Für die spezifischen Funk-tionen sind im Entwurf keine unterschiedlichen Gebäu-detypen vorgesehen.

The plan consists, in essence, of a system of building alignments, attuned to the proportions of the existing street pattern and buildings. Within the "structure," it will be possible to accommodate, in addition to the buildings that are to be retained, different building types and also different functions. This will happin, in practice, over a longer period of time and in a much more varied way than can be indicated in a plan. The overall plan may thus be compared with an urban fabric consisting of a warp and weft. If we conceive of the final result as a woven fabric, then what we can design represents only the weft threads; the warp is then constituted by the specific needs as they arise from practical usage. There has not been de-signed a different type of building for each specifically de-signed function.

Bestehende Situation mit Kühlturm /
Existing situation with cooling tower

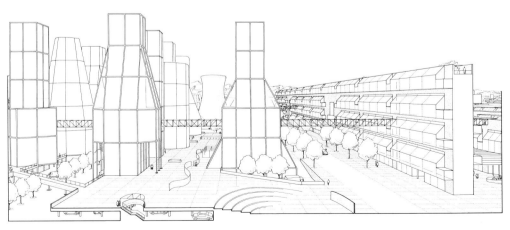

Bereich mit Türmen /
Area with towers

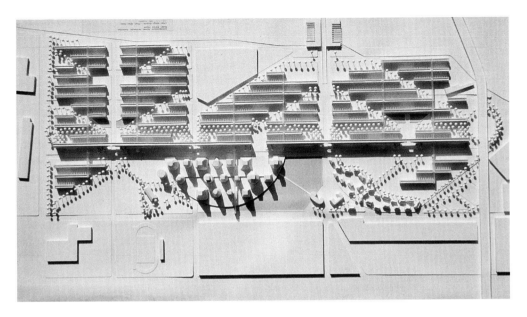

Modell / Model

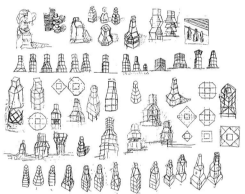

Turmstudien /
Study towers

Giorgio Morandi (1890–1964):
«Stilleben mit weisser Teekanne» (1956).
Kunstmuseum Winterthur. /
"Still life with white teapot" (1956).
Art Museum Winterthur.

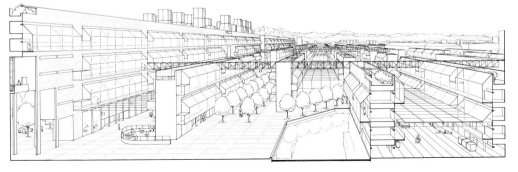

Bereich mit Gebäudezeilen /
Area with building slabs

Gemäldegalerie
Projekt, Berlin, 1986

Museum for Paintings
Project, Berlin, Germany, 1986

Das Projekt ist der Entwurf zu einem Erweiterungsbau des bestehenden Museumskomplexes auf dem Berliner Kulturforum. Die Galerie hat die Form einer Landschaft aus langgestreckten, von parallelen Wänden flankierten Promenaden-Räumen. Die «Promenaden» liegen in einem Höhenabstand von 50 cm schräg übereinander und sind durch Stufen und Rampen verbunden. Der Hauptverbindungsweg bietet gewissermaßen einen Querschnitt durch die gesamte Museumslandschaft und vermittelt dem Besucher bereits beim Eintritt einen Gesamteindruck von der Sammlung. Ein Gang durch die Promenaden erschließt die Bestände in chronologischer Ordnung. Schlägt man durch die hohen vertikalen Wandöffnungen hindurch die Seitenwege ein, ergibt sich ein Querschnitt durch die Jahrhunderte.

This project entails the design of an extension to the existing museum complex situated on the Kulturforum in Berlin. The painting galleries take the form of a landscape of elongated avenue spaces with parallel walls. The successive "avenues", connected with steps and ramps, are situated on an incline so that each is 50 cm higher than the preceding one. The main connecting walkway provides a cross-section of the entire museum landscape, as it were, thereby enabling the visitor to gain an overall impression of the collection upon entering. By following the direction of the avenues, the collection can be viewed chronologically. By taking the side ways through the high vertical openings in the wall, one is given a cross-section through time.

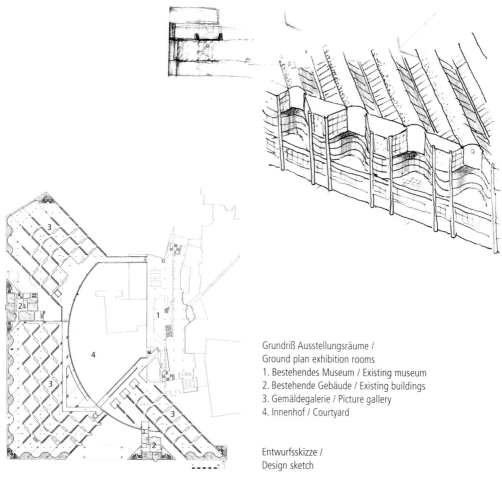

Grundriß Ausstellungsräume /
Ground plan exhibition rooms
1. Bestehendes Museum / Existing museum
2. Bestehende Gebäude / Existing buildings
3. Gemäldegalerie / Picture gallery
4. Innenhof / Courtyard

Entwurfsskizze /
Design sketch

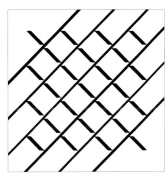

Schema der Sichtachsen in drei Richtungen /
Schemes with view lines in three directions

Modell / Model

Schnitt Ausstellungsgalerien /
Exhibition galleries, section

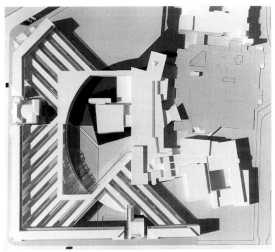

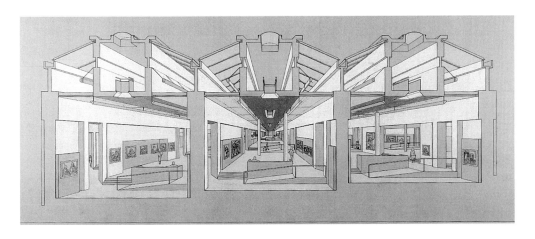

Schule. Erweiterung
Aerdenhout, 1988–1989

School. Extension
Aerdenhout, 1988–1989

Der Erweiterungsbau ersetzt einen Flügel mit Klassenzimmern, die zuvor an einen Korridor stießen. Ein Teil des alten Gebäudes blieb erhalten. Der alte Teil und die neuen Ergänzungen sind in Form und Material völlig verschieden. Bei der Erweiterung wurde den städtebaulichen Gegebenheiten in besonderer Weise Rechnung getragen. Vier Klassenzimmer liegen in einem Halbzylinder, einem zweigeschossigen Baukörper, der die Krümmung der Straßenkurve aufnimmt. Ein rechteckiger Block, der sich formal an die benachbarten Villen anlehnt, bietet Raum für die übrigen Klassenzimmer. Zwischen den neuen Gebäudeteilen und dem Rest des Altbaus dient ein keilförmiges Vestibül als Haupteingang und Gemeinschaftsraum für Veranstaltungen. Es ermöglicht darüber hinaus den Lichteinfall ins Gebäude und in die Klassenzimmer, die durch Glaswände vom Gebäudeinneren abgetrennt sind.

The extension replaces the wing with the classrooms, which were formerly placed along a corridor. Part of the old building has been maintained. The old and the new parts are completely different in form and material. The new extension deals in a particular way with the urbanistic setting. Four classrooms are placed in a semi-cylindrical and two storey high volume, which follows the curve of the street. The other classrooms are in a rectangular block that takes up the form of the villas in the neighbourhood. Between these parts and the remains of the old building, a wedge-shaped hall serves as main entrance and common space where events can take place. This construction also allows light to pour into the building and to the classrooms which are separated from it by glass walls.

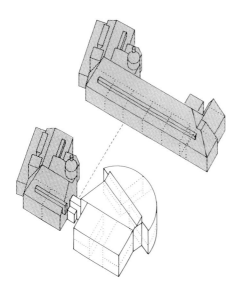

Teilansicht Fassade / Partial view facade
Gebäude vor und nach der Erweiterung, Schema /
Building before and after the extension, scheme
Ausgangsidee für den Entwurf / Initial idea for the design
Situationsplan / Site plan
Ansicht nach der Erweiterung / View after the the extension

0 10   20m

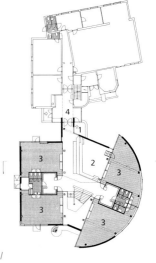

1. Eingang / Entrance
2. Gemeinschaftsraum /
   Communal space
3. Klassenzimmer /
   Classroom
4. Bestehendes Gebäude /
   Existing building

Zentrale Treppe / Central staircase

Grundriß Erdgeschoß / Ground floor plan

Ansicht Neubau / View of the new building

Schnitt / Section

Zentrale Halle / Central hall

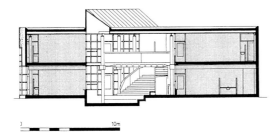

10m

Bibliothèque de France
Wettbewerb, Paris, 1989

Zu seinem Projekt schrieb der Architekt: «Der neue Bibliotheksbau soll nicht nur eine kulturelle Mahlzeit anrichten, sondern auch den Appetit darauf wecken. Den größten Teil des Gebäudes nimmt eine glasgedeckte Halle ein, die größer ist als das Grand Palais. Die Halle bildet das große Dach, unter dem, geparkt wie riesige Lastwagen, Container oder Eisenbahnzüge, die langezogenen Rechtecke der verschiedenen Bibliothekseinheiten Platz finden. Diese geparkten Objekte haben die Größe der Bibliothèque Ste. Geneviève.» Die mehrfach kombinierbaren Bibliothekseinheiten umschließen den öffentlichen Bereich. Er läßt sich als gedeckter städtischer Platz betrachten und bietet alle Möglichkeiten eines solchen sowie Raum für Ausstellungen. Von diesem Platz aus lassen sich wie auf einem gut organisierten Flughafen sämtliche Eingänge zu den verschiedenen Abteilungen überblicken.

Bibliothèque de France
Competition, Paris, 1989

As the architect writes: "The new library should not only serve up cultural repast but create an appetite for it too. The building consists mainly of a glass covered hall, which in terms of scale surpasses the Grand Palais. This hall forms the great roof under which the various oblong library units are placed, parked like enormous trucks, containers, or trains. These parked objects have the size of the Bibliothèque Ste. Geneviève." In between the library units, which can function in varying combinations, is the public space that can be regarded as a covered town square with all urban facilities possible and room for exhibitions. From this square one can see all of the entrances to the different sections, like at a well-organized airport.

Skizze der glasgedeckten Halle /
Sketch of the glass-covered hall

Modelle / Models

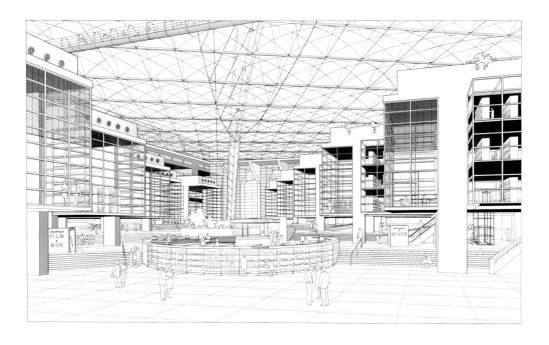

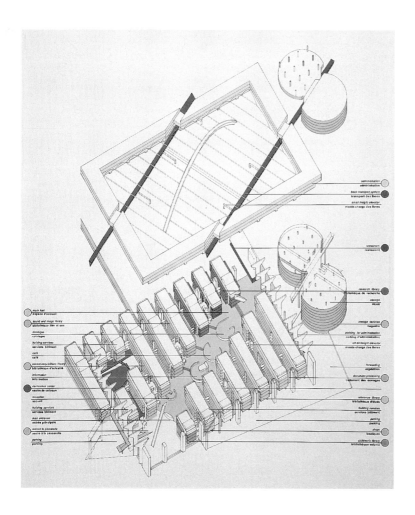

main hall
espace d'accueil

sound and image library
bibliothèque film et son

catalogue
catalogue

building services
services bâtiment

café
café

recent acquisitions library
bibliothèque d'actualité

information
information

conference center
centre de colloque

reception
accueil

building services
services bâtiment

main entrance
entrée principale

access to passerelle
accès à la passerelle

parking
parking

administration
administration

book transport system
transport des livres

small freight elevator
monte-charge des livres

restaurant
restaurant

research library
bibliothèque de recherche

storage
dépôt

storage facilities
magasins

parking for administration
parking d'administration

small freight elevator
monte-charge des livres

forwarding
expédition

document processing
traitement des ouvrages

reference library
bibliothèque d'étude

building services
services bâtiment

parking
parking

shops
boutiques

children's library
bibliothèque enfants

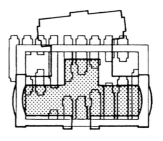

Axonometrieschema / Axonometric scheme

Grand Palais, Paris

Größenvergleich mit dem Grand Palais in Paris /
Size in comparison to the Grand Palais in Paris

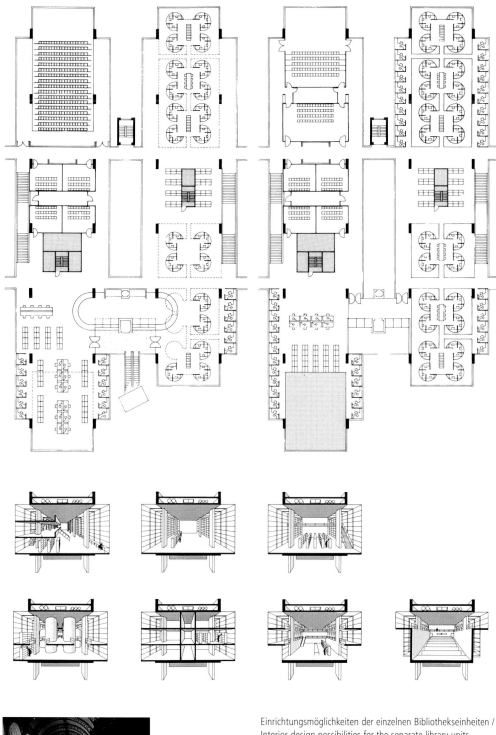

Einrichtungsmöglichkeiten der einzelnen Bibliothekseinheiten /
Interior design possibilities for the separate library units

Bibliothèque S. Geneviève, Paris,
als Beispiel für eine Bibliothekseinheit. /
The Bibliothèque S. Geneviève in Paris
as an example for a library unit.

Kulturzentrum am See
mit Konzertsälen
Wettbewerb, Luzern, Schweiz 1989

Cultural Center with Concert Building
on the Lake
Competition, Luzern, Switzerland, 1989

Die wunderbare Lage des Baugeländes am See, im Herzen der Stadt, wo sich der Blick auf das Alpenpanorama erschließt, führte zu der Idee, einen eindrücklichen Schlußakzent zu setzen – dem Seeufer eine neue Begrenzung zu geben. Der Baukörper wurde aus der Form der verschiedenen Konzertsäle entwickelt, die, zum Viertelkreis gereiht, seewärts ansteigen. Das Gebäude erhält auf diese Weise einen fächerförmigen Abschluß, der sich virtuell über das Ufer hinaus bis auf die Wasserfläche fortzusetzen scheint. Der zentrale öffentliche Bereich, Foyer und Treppen, ist den Konzertsälen seeseitig vorgelagert und bietet damit einen prachtvollen Ausblick auf die Stadt und den See. Für die Besucher, die sich die Schiffe anschauen wollen oder nach Schiffspassagieren an den Landestellen Ausschau halten, ist zusätzlich eine Fußgängerzone zwischen See und Gebäude vorgesehen. Die Dampfer auf dem See bildeten eine wichtige visuelle Anregung für das allgemeine Konzept des Entwurfs.

The beautiful building site in the heart of the city, on the waterfront with a panoramic view of the Alps, led to create a special termination point and to provide a new edge at the side of the lake. The building was developed out of the shape of the different auditoriums, which mount in a curve towards the lake. The building thus has a fanshaped conclusion which wants to project over the water. The main public area, the foyer and the stairs, run along these auditoriums and permit a magnificent view of the lake and the city. Between the building and the water, a pedestrian zone provides extra space for those who want to look at the boats and for the ships' passengers at the landings. The boats on the lake formed an important image source for the general concept of the plan.

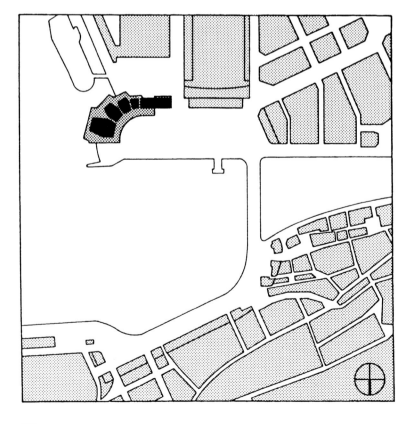

Schema Situation /
Site plan

Modell / Model

Grundriß Foyer /
Foyer floor plan

Schnitt / Section

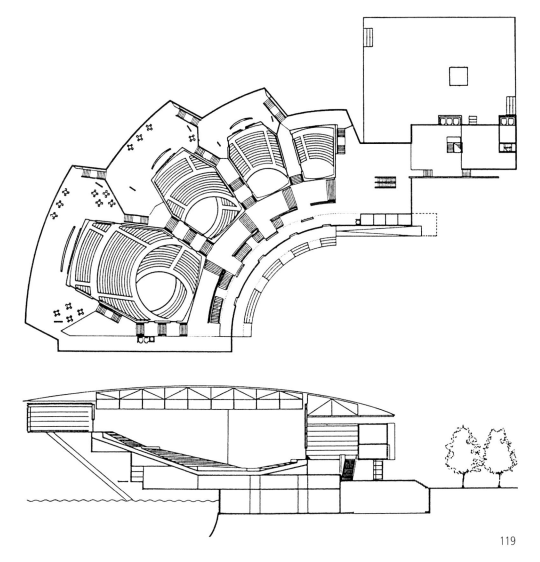

Wohnhäuser
Almere, 1989–1990 und 1990–1992

Der Entwurf für de Muziekwijk (Typ A) umfaßt 16 Wohnungen, auf vier Gruppen von je vier zusammenhängenden Wohnhäusern verteilt. Jedem Grundriß liegt ein Quadrat von 8 x 8 Metern zugrunde, von dem eine Ecke ausgespart bleibt. Auf diese Weise entsteht ein Außenraum, der durch eine Glaswand in den Wohnbereich einbezogen ist. Bis auf den festgelegten Grundbereich bleibt die Gestaltung der Stockwerke den Wünschen der Bewohner überlassen. Auch die Häuser in de Filmwijk (Typ B) haben einen offenen Grundriß. Das diagonal plazierte Wohnzimmer hat eine maximale Länge von 12 Metern. Die halb freistehenden Häuser verfügen über ein gewisses Maß an Autonomie.

Housing
Almere, 1989–1990 and 1990–1992

The plan of de Muziekwijk (type A) contains 16 dwellings divided into 4 groups of 4 connected residences. Each floor plan is a square of 8 x 8 meters of which one corner is left open. In this way, an outside space is created which is connected by a glass wall to the living room. Except for the fixed core, the layout of the floors can be arranged according to the desires of the inhabitants. The houses in de Filmwijk (type B) also have an open floor plan. The diagonally situated living room has a maximum length of 12 meters. The semi-detachment gives the houses a certain autonomy.

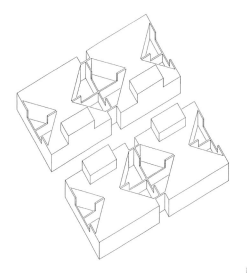

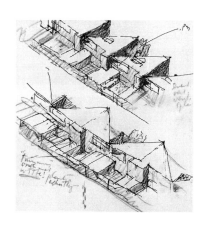

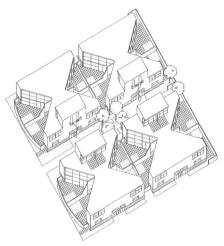

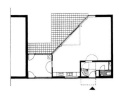

Axonometrie Typ A / Axometric view type A

Skizze Typ B / Sketch type B

Städtebauliche Lösung mit verschiedenen Kombinationen von
Wohneinheiten der Typen A und B /
Urban solution with different combinations of living units of
the types A and B

Ansicht Typ A / View type A
Ansicht Typ B / View type B
Grundriß Typ A / Ground plan type A
Grundriß Typ B / Ground plan type B

Media-Park. Gebäudekomplex mit Wohnungen, Studios und Büros
Wettbewerb, 1. Preis, Köln, 1990

Media Park. Building with Housing, Studios and Offices
Competition, first prize, Cologne, Germany, 1990

Die einzelnen Blocks sind nicht entlang der Baulinie angeordnet, sondern wie Tortenstücke gruppiert, deren Spitzen auf einen runden Platz weisen. Die nach innen gerichteten Straßenfronten sind wie Fassaden behandelt. Die «Haut» der Blocksegmente ist dick genug, um Standardbüros aufzunehmen. Sie enthält Ausbuchtungen, deren jede sich nach Bedarf ausfüllen läßt. Diese eingekapselten Räume sind hinter einen Fassadenraster gelegt, der, von den Hauptstraßen her betrachtet, ein einheitliches Bild garantiert. Der Raum im Mittelpunkt des Block-Komplexes ist von allen Seiten her zugänglich und wird dadurch zu einem öffentlichen Durchgang.

The blocks are not placed along the building line, but arranged like wedges of cake pointing towards a round square. The frontages, looking inward, are treated like facades. The segments which form the block consist of a skin which is thick enough to accommodate standard offices. Inside this skin are spaces ("paunches"), each of which can be filled in as circumstances require. These encapsulated spaces lay behind grid structures that guarantee unity when seen from the main streets. The central space left between the segments is accessible on all sides and has thus become a public passage.

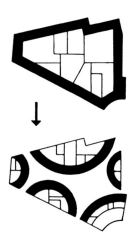

Entwurfsskizzen /
Design sketches

Schema, das Innere richtet
sich nach Außen. /
Scheme with the inside
oriented towards the outside.

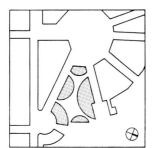

Situationsplan /
Site plan

Modell mit Glasdach /
Model with glass roof

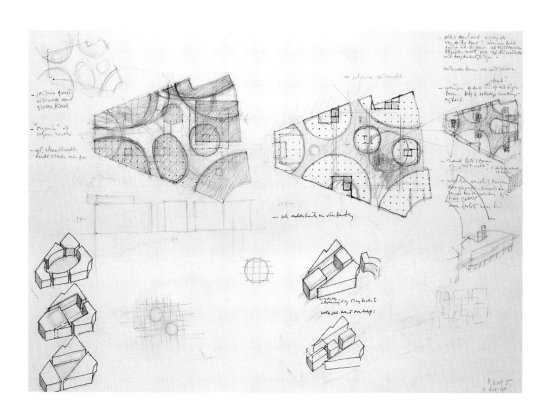

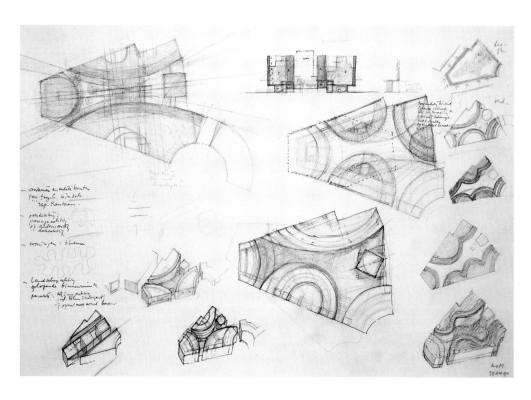

124

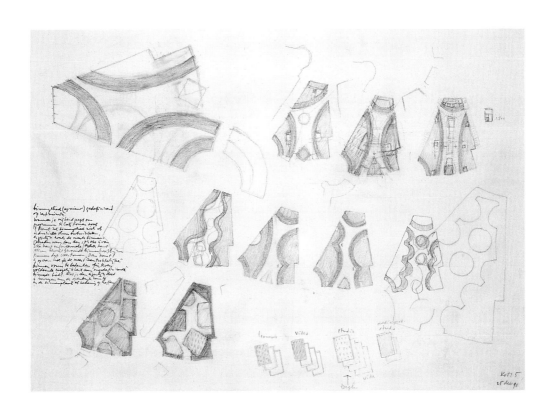

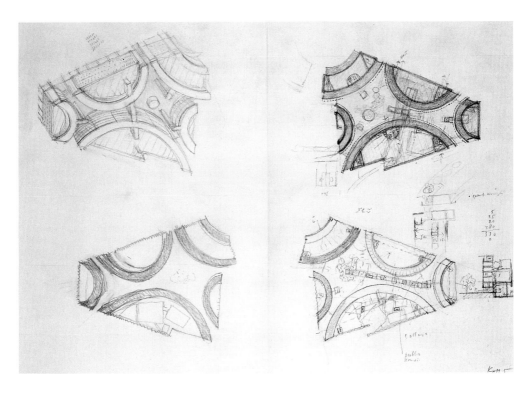

Entwurfsskizzen / Design sketches

Kindergarten und Schule De Polygoon
Almere, 1990–1992

Die Schule besteht aus zwei Trakten, von denen der eine die Klassenzimmer enthält, der zweite und höhere die Verwaltungsräume, eine Turnhalle und ein Spielzimmer. Die Einheiten sind unterschiedlich ausgeführt. An ihrer Nahtstelle bildet ein Foyer einen Gemeinschaftsraum, der auch als Amphitheater genutzt werden kann. Die sechzehn Klassenzimmer sind nicht um eine Indoor-Piazza angeordnet, sondern säumen die Seiten eines langgestreckten Raumbandes. In der Mitte dieser «Straße» sind wie eine Kette von Arbeitsinseln zusätzliche Unterrichtszimmer aufgereiht, die für räumliche Differenzierung sorgen. Zwischen den Arbeitsinseln liegen offene Zonen, von denen jede vier Klassenzimmern zur Verfügung steht. Eine durchlaufende Reihe von Oberlichtern versorgt die Straße in ihrer ganzen Länge mit Tageslicht.

De Polygoon Kindergarten and School
Almere, 1990–1992

The school consists of two blocks: one which houses the classrooms and a taller one with the administration offices, a gym and a playroom. Each block has been treated differently. At their junction, a hall serves as common space which can be used as an amphitheater. The sixteen classrooms are not arranged around a central indoor square but along an elongated space. In the middle of this "street", supplementary instruction rooms are placed like a train of working islands, giving it a spatial differentiation. In between the working islands are open areas which serve four classrooms each. The entire length of the street is flooded with daylight through a continuous strip of skylights.

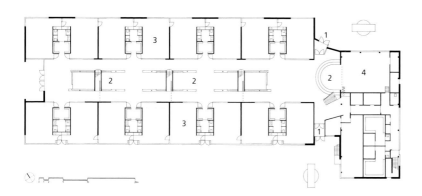

Grundriß / Ground plan
1. Eingang / Entrance
2. Zentrale «Straße» /
   Central "street"
3. Klassenzimmer /
   Classroom
4. Spielraum / Playroom

Südwestfassade /
Southwest facade

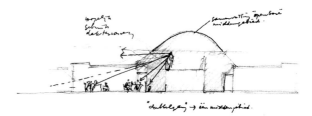

Westfassade /
West facade

Schnitt /
Section

Ostfassade /
East facade

Zentrale Halle / Central hall

Innenerker der Klassenräume /
Bay windows of the classrooms

Die zentrale Halle wird vielfältig genutzt. /
The central hall ist used in many different ways.

Benelux Merkenbureau. Bürogebäude
Den Haag, 1990–1993

Benelux Merkenbureau Office Building
The Hague, 1990–1993

Ein Bürohaus der üblichen Art wurde mit Hilfe eines einfachen Gestaltungsverfahrens so aufgebrochen, daß anstelle der Flure Foyers entstehen und alle Räume an zwei Atrien stoßen, von denen der Blick nach draußen ins Grüne fällt. Dieses Vorgehen befreite den Bau vom traditionellen Image des Bürogebäudes mit langen, von Zimmerreihen flankierten Korridoren. Verläßt man ein Büro, überblickt man das ganze Hausinnere und kann gleichzeitig Kontakt mit Kollegen aufnehmen. Der zentrale Bereich, der die Binnenstruktur räumlich definiert und die verschiedenen Stockwerke verbindet, ist charakteristisch für das Gebäude als Ganzes: er stimuliert soziale Kontakte.

With a simple design procedure the common standard office building was broken open so that the corridors become halls and all the rooms are grouped along two atria which permit a view on the outside green space. This liberated the building from the traditional image of an office building with long corridors which have rooms on both sides. Coming out of the room one can oversee the entire building and, at the same time, interact with co-workers. The central area, which defines the internal organization spatially and connects the different floors, is characteristic for the building as a whole. It stimulates social contacts.

Nordansicht /
North elevation

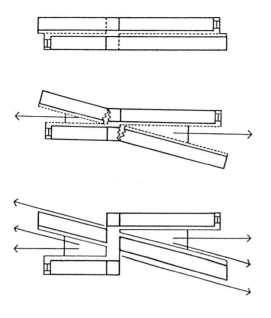

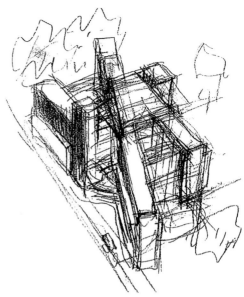

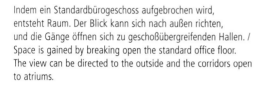

Indem ein Standardbürogeschoss aufgebrochen wird, entsteht Raum. Der Blick kann sich nach außen richten, und die Gänge öffnen sich zu geschoßübergreifenden Hallen. / Space is gained by breaking open the standard office floor. The view can be directed to the outside and the corridors open to atriums.

Entwurfsskizze / Design sketch

Westansicht /
West elevation

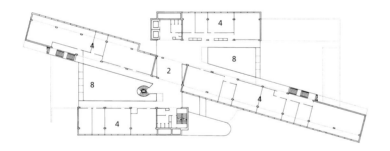

Grundriß erstes Obergeschoß /
1st floor ground plan

Grundriß Erdgeschoß /
Ground floor plan

1. Eingang / Entrance
2. Halle / Hall
3. Empfang / Reception
4. Büro / Office
5. Restaurant / Restaurant
6. Küche / Kitchen
7. Terrasse / Terrace
8. Luftraum / Air space

Entwurfsskizze /
Design sketch

Zentrale Halle /
Central hall

Zentrale Halle, Detail /
Central hall, detail

Centraal Beheer. Erweiterung
Apeldoorn, 1990–1995

Ursprünglich bestand Centraal Beheer aus dem Originalgebäude von 1972 und einem anstoßenden Bürotrakt (Architekten: Kaman und Davidse), mit dem es durch eine Passerelle verbunden war. Die verschiedenen Abteilungen ließen sich zwar durch zahlreiche Eingänge erreichen, doch fehlte die Erschließung durch einen nennenswerten zentralen Raum. Der zwischen den beiden Bauten eingeschobene Erweiterungsbau bildet ein neues Gebäudezentrum mit Tagungsräumen und ist durch einen neuen Eingang von der Zugangsstraße her erschlossen. Sein Hauptzweck ist die Bewältigung der wachsenden Besucherzahlen. Der neue Eingang führt in einen langgestreckten Baukörper – im wesentlichen ein glasgedecktes Atrium –, den Hauptempfangsbereich des Gesamtgebäudes. Ein freistehender «Indoor-Bau» innerhalb des Atriums enthält verschiedene Tagungsräume, einschließlich eines bescheidenen, doch vollständig ausgestatteten Konferenzsaals.

Centraal Beheer. Extension
Apeldoorn, 1990–1995

Centraal Beheer used to consist of the original building dating from 1972 and the adjoining office (architects: Kaman and Davidse) linked by a overhead passageway. There were many entrances and no central space to speak of from which to reach the various departments. The new extension combines an additional feature set between the two buildings to establish a new center with meeting facilities and a new entrance on the access road, principally to cope with the increase in the number of visitors. This new entrance opens onto an elongated volume, essentially an atrium roofed in glass. Here we find the main reception area of the entire building. Set in this atrium is a freestanding "indoor building" with a variety of meeting facilities, including a modest, though complete, conference center.

Grundriß /
Ground floor plan
1. Eingang / Entrance
2. Rezeption / Reception
3. Atrium / Atrium
4. Auskunft /
   Information desk
5. Konferenzraum /
   Conference hall
6. Sitzungsraum /
   Meeting room

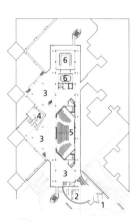

Eingangshalle / Entrance hall

Situationsplan / Site plan

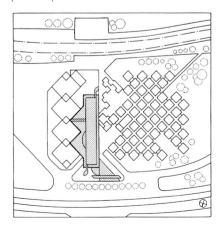

134

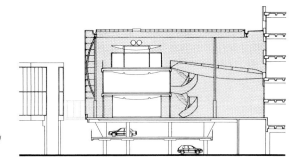

Schnitt / Section

Ansicht der Stirnfassade /
View front facade

Atrium / Atrium

Treppe im Atrium / Staircase in the atrium

Bibliothek und Zentrum für Kunst und Musik
Breda, 1991–1993

Der Gebäudekomplex schiebt sich weit in einen alten Hof vor, von dem als Restbestand ein kleiner Garten mit einigen Maulbeerbäumen überlebt hat. Zur Molenstraat hin, wo der Haupteingang liegt, nimmt ein weitläufiges Dach die gekrümmte Baulinie auf. Unter diesem Dach hängt die Musikschule wie ein gestreckter Quader über dem Raum, in dem Bibliothek und Lesesaal ineinander übergehen. Die Räume sowie die als Baummetaphern gestalteten Stahlstützen sind von der Straße her sichtbar. Das Gebäudeinnere ist betont durchlässig gehalten. Hinter der stärker abgeschlossenen Fassade gegen Oude Veste, eine Hauptverkehrsstraße, liegen die Musikstudios und die Büroräume.

Library and Center for Art and Music
Breda, 1991–1993

The building complex penetrates deep into an old courtyard, leaving only a small garden around some mulberry trees. On the Molenstraat, where the main entrance is, the building has been covered by a large roof that follows the original curved building line. Under this roof the music school hangs like an oblong box above the undivided space of the library and reading room. From the street one can see these spaces and the steel columns which refer metaphorically to the form of trees. The inside of the building is kept very transparent. Behind the more closed facade, towards the Oude Veste, a major traffic street, are the music studios and the offices.

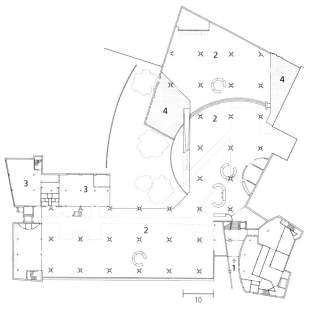

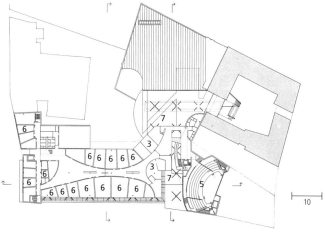

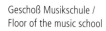

Geschoß Musikschule /
Floor of the music school

Geschoß Bibliothek /
Library floor

1. Eingang Bibliothek und Musikschule /
   Entrance library and music school
2. Bibliotheksraum / Library space
3. Büro / Office
4. Innenhof / Courtyard
5. Musiksaal / Music hall
6. Musikstudio / Music studio
7. Luftraum / Air space

Situationsplan /
Site plan

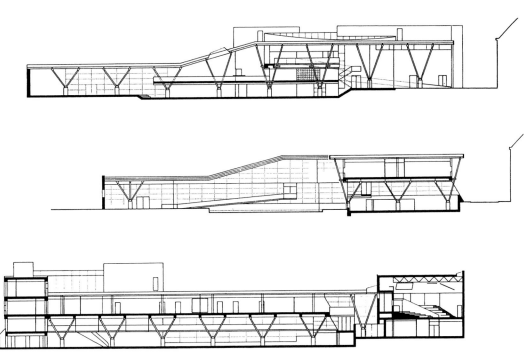

Fassade zum Innengarten /
Inner garden facade

Schnitte / Sections

Lichthof Bibliotheksraum / Light yard library

Blick in den Garten / View of the garden

Straßenfassade von innen und außen / Street facade from the inside and outside

Musikzentrum
Projekt, Amsterdam, 1992

Music Center
Project, Amsterdam, 1992

Das Projekt ist mehr als ein Gebäude – es versammelt Möglichkeiten. Die Raumanordnung ist so gewählt, daß das Gebäude unterschiedlich genutzt werden kann. Die verschiedenen Funktionen sind zu autonomen Zonen zusammengefaßt: Probenräume, Hinterbühne, Konzertsäle und Foyerbereich. Mit Hilfe technischer Einrichtungen lassen sich verschiedene Kombinationen herstellen. An der Außenseite ist das Gebäude hauptsächlich durch den Wechsel von flachen und gewölbten Dachflächen differenziert.

More than a building, this project is a carrier of possibilities. The spatial disposition is thus chosen so that a number of facilities can be located in the building. These facilities are grouped into autonomous sections which contain: the rehearsal rooms, the backstage passage, the concert halls and the foyer area. With the help of technical devices, different combinations can be achieved. On the outside the building has been differentiated mainly by the alternation of flat and curved roofs.

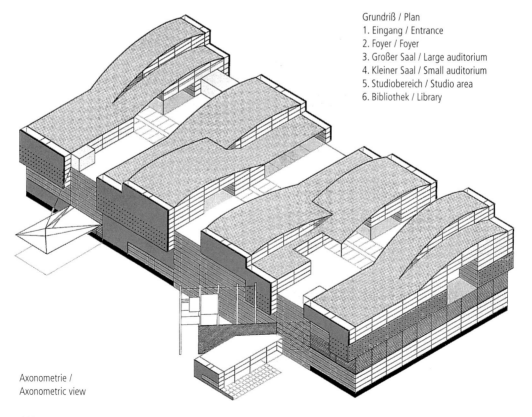

Grundriß / Plan
1. Eingang / Entrance
2. Foyer / Foyer
3. Großer Saal / Large auditorium
4. Kleiner Saal / Small auditorium
5. Studiobereich / Studio area
6. Bibliothek / Library

Axonometrie /
Axonometric view

Modell / Model

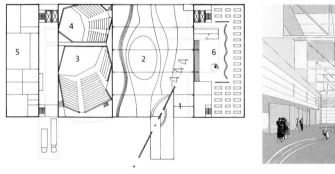

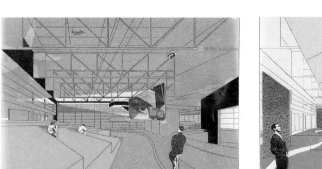

Perspektivische Skizzen der Haupthalle /
Sketches in perspective of the main hall

Chassé-Theater
Breda, 1992–1995

Das Gebäude liegt zwischen einer alten Kaserne und einer kommunalen Behörde auf einem wenig markanten Gelände, das sich unmittelbar an das historische Ortszentrum anschließt. Um einen Vorplatz zu schaffen, wurde das Gebäude von der Baulinie zurückgesetzt. Die beiden Bühnentürme, die das Gebäude zu einem dominierenden Element im Stadtbild gemacht hätten, deckt ein riesiges gewelltes Dach, dessen zweiter, tieferliegender Teil auch über das Foyer und die Kinosäle gezogen ist. So tritt kein Teil des Gebäudes nach außen auffällig in Erscheinung, und das Dach ist zur Hauptfassade geworden. Das Foyer, das als Straße durch das Gebäude geführt wird, liegt seitlich der Theatersäle und wird durch Treppen und Übergänge sowie durch die farbigen Dachstützen belebt. Da die drei Zuschauersäle für die Besucher nur von einer Seite her zugänglich sind, wurde der größte der drei Säle durch zahlreiche Balkone in unterschiedlicher Größe und Form asymmetrisch gestaltet.

Chassé Theater
Breda, 1992–1995

The building is located on a hardly characteristic site just outside the historical center of Breda between an old barracks and a municipal office. The theater is set back from the building line in order to create a forecourt. The two flytowers, which would have dominated the image of the building in the cityscape, are covered by a huge undulating roof which has been split and also covers the foyer and the film auditoriums. Thus, no part of the building reveals itself prominently at the outside, and the roof has become the main facade of the building. The foyer, which penetrates the building as a street, is placed at one side of the theater auditoriums and is enlivened with staircases and bridges and by the colored columns which sustain the roof. The fact that the theater-going public can approach the three auditoriums only from one side has led to an asymmetrical organization of the main auditorium, with many balconies each of its own size and shape.

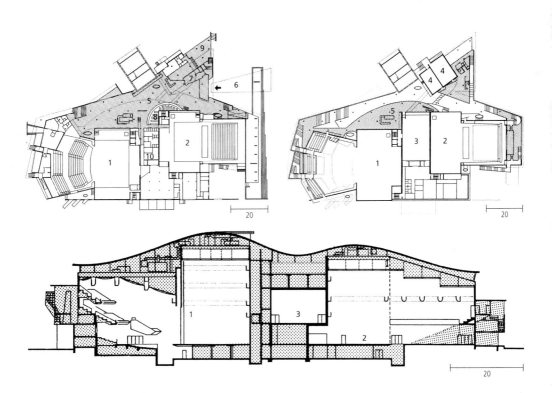

Rückfront mit Treppenaufgang zum Großen Saal /
Rear facade with stairs to the large auditorium

Grundriß Erdgeschoß / Ground floor plan
Grundriß erstes Obergeschoß / 1st floor ground plan
Schnitt / Section

1. Großer Theatersaal / Large auditorium
2. Kleiner Theatersaal / Small auditorium
3. Studio / Studio
4. Kino / Cinema
5. Foyer / Foyer
6. Eingang / Entrance
7. Theaterkasse / Ticket office
8. Garderobe / Cloakroom
9. Café / Café

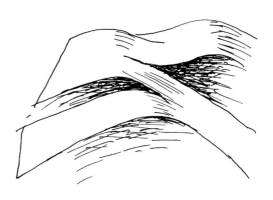

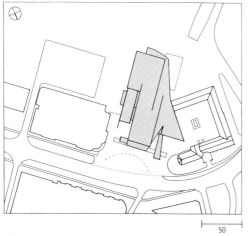

Innenansicht des Großen Saals /
Interior of the large auditorium

Skizze Dachform /
Sketch roof form

Situationsplan /
Site plan

Foyer mit Kinosälen / Foyer with cinema

Alberto Giacometti (1906-1966), «Femme couchée qui rêve» (1929). Alberto Giacometti – Stiftung, Zürich. / Alberto Giacometti Foundation, Zurich.

Konstruktionsprinzip des Daches / Construction principle of the roof

Integration ins Stadtbild / Integration into the existing cityscape

Treppen am Notausgang / Emergency exit stairs

Südansicht / View from the south

Nordansicht / View from the north

Innenansichten des Foyers / Interior views of the foyer

Anne-Frank-Schule und Wohnbau
Papendrecht, 1993–1996

Die Grundschule mit acht Klassenzimmern bildet einen städtebaulichen Eckstein in einem Gelände, das durch Wohnbauten erschlossen werden soll. Das Gebäude ist vertikal akzentuiert, um es von seiner zukünftigen Umgebung abzuheben. Die Klassenräume liegen in zwei identisch ausgeführten Gebäudetrakten, die übrigen Räume in einem dritten, um ein Halbgeschoß erhöhten Teil. Zwischen den drei Blöcken liegt das Foyer – das Herz des Gebäudes und der Konvergenzpunkt aller Aktivitäten. Die Krümmung der Dächer über der Halle soll eine narrative Wirkung schaffen und außerdem Richtung und Höhe der verschiedenen Volumen bündeln.

Anne Frank School and Housing
Papendrecht, 1993–1996

This school of eight classes provides an urban cornerstone for a site otherwise destined for housing development. It has been given a vertical treatment that serves to separate it from its future neighbours. The classes occupy two identical blocks, whereas the other rooms are in a third block that has been lifted half a level. In between these blocks is the central hall, which is the heart of the building where all activity converges. The hall is covered by curved roofs in order to create a narrative effect and to unite the directional lines and heights of the surrounding masses.

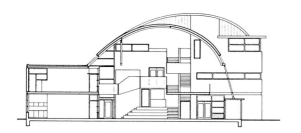

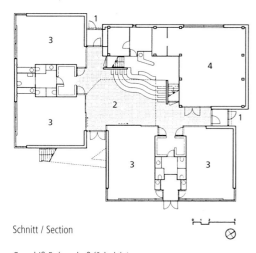

Schnitt / Section

Grundriß Erdgeschoß (Schule) /
Ground floor plan (school)
1. Eingang / Entrance
2. Gemeinschaftsraum / Communal space
3. Klassenzimmer / Classroom
4. Spielraum / Playroom

Situationsschema / Site diagram

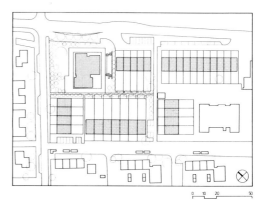

Ansicht Schule und Wohnungen / View school and housing

Schnitt und
Grundrisse
Wohnungen /
Apartments,
section and
ground plans

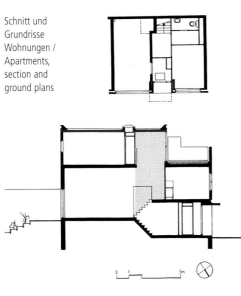

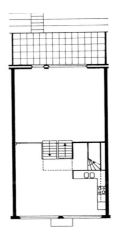

Vorderfassade Wohnungen / Housing, front facades

Hinterfassade Wohnungen / Housing, rear facades

155

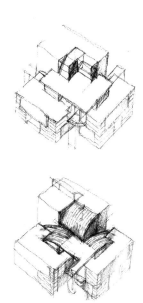

Eingangsseite
mit Schulhof /
Entrance side
with schoolyard

Treppen in der
zentralen Halle /
Stairs in central hall

Entwurfsskizzen /
Design sketches

Innenansichten der zentralen Halle / Interior views of central hall

Innenansichten der zentralen Halle / Interior views of the central hall

Ansicht Gartenseite mit Fluchttreppe / View with emergency stairs towards the garden

Ansicht Straßenseite / View from the street

De-Bombardon-Schule
Almere, 1993–1995

De Bombardon School
Almere, 1993–1995

Die Schule ist für Kinder mit Lern- und Verhaltensproblemen bestimmt. Sie enthält 14 Klassenzimmer und zahlreiche weitere Räume für Bewegungstherapie, Förderunterricht und ähnliches. Da es in erster Linie darum ging, ohne Korridore auszukommen, stoßen alle Räume an den Innenhof, einen leicht erhöhten Platz, der durch einige Stufen gebildet wird. Er kann den unterschiedlichsten Zwecken dienen; die Treppen verleihen ihm einen dynamischen Zug. Das Schulgebäude ist sehr kompakt gehalten. Die Turnhalle ist fast vollständig in den Haupttrakt geschoben. Im ersten Stock läuft eine Galerie rund um das Schulgebäude, die von den Kindern als Pausenspielplatz genutzt werden kann.

The school for children with learning and educational problems comprises of 14 classrooms and a large amount of additional rooms for movement therapy, remedial teaching, etc. The main issue was to avoid corridors. Therefore, all of the rooms open onto an inner school square. This elevated space, which has been articulated by a few steps, can be used for all kinds of activities. The stairs add a dynamic touch. The building is kept rather compact; the gym has been pushed almost completely into the main block. A gallery runs around the school on the first floor, which can be used by the children during playtime.

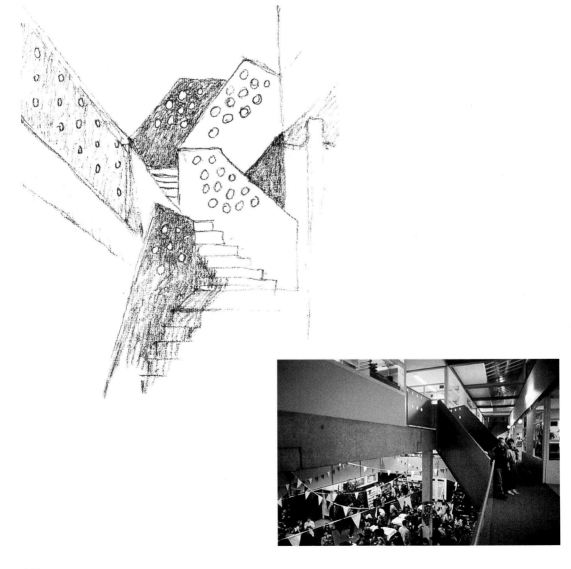

Entwurfsskizze /
Design sketch

Halle als Gemeinschaftsraum /
Hall as communal area

Schnitt / Section

Galerie / Gallery

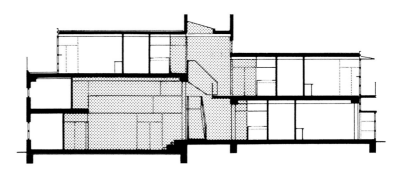

Ansicht Südfassade / View south facade

Grundriß Erdgeschoß / Ground floor plan
Grundriß erstes Obergeschoß / 1st floor plan
Grundriß zweites Obergeschoß / 2nd floor plan
1. Eingang / Entrance
2. Gemeinschaftsraum / Communal space
3. Klassenzimmer / Classroom
4. Turnhalle / Gym
5. Spielraum / Playroom

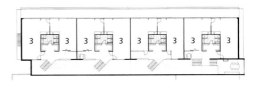

Markant Theater
Uden, 1993–1996

Das neue Gebäude sollte sich in eine bestehende Straßenfront einfügen und darum nicht zu kolossal wirken. Aus diesem Grund wurde es in kleineren Elementen ausgeführt. Der einladend gestaltete Haupteingang schließt sich an eine weitflächige Glaswand an, hinter der das Foyer liegt. Ein auskragendes Vordach überdeckt den Bereich zwischen der zurückgesetzten Glaswand und der Straßenfront, der so zu einem Übergangsraum, halb Straße und halb Gebäude, wird. Dieser Vorraum bindet das Gebäude in den öffentlichen Raum ein. Das Theater ist kein in sich geschlossener Raum: es öffnet sich und zieht zugleich an. Nachts wirkt der Foyerbereich um den Zuschauerraum wie ein Leuchtsignal.

Markant Theater
Uden, 1993–1996

The new building had to become a part of an existing street wall. Therefore, it should not appear too colossal. This is the reason why the building has been articulated in smaller elements. The main entrance has been given an inviting form next to a large glass front, behind which there is the foyer. A large awning covers the area between the retreating glass theater wall and the street front. This area thus becomes part of the street and part of the building. It is the urban porch which makes the building penetrate in the public realm. The theater is not a formal and closed building, but an open and attractive one. At night, the foyer space around the auditorium serves as a beacon.

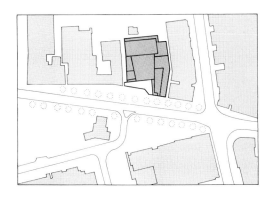

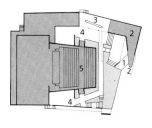
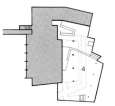
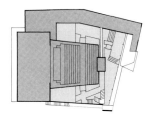
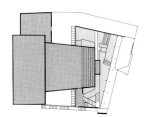

Eingangsfassade /
Entrance facade

Situationsplan /
Site plan

Grundriß Erdgeschoß /
Ground floor plan
1. Eingang / Entrance
2. Büro / Office
3. Garderobe / Cloakroom
4. Foyer / Foyer
5. Theatersaal / Auditorium

Grundriß Souterrain /
Semibasement plan

Grundriß 1. Obergeschoß /
1st floor plan

Grundriß 2. Obergeschoß /
2nd floor plan

Foyer / Foyer

Fassadenschnitt /
Section facade

Schnitt / Section

Fassade bei Beleuchtung /
Facade at night

Foyer mit Galerien /
Foyer with galleries

Aufgang zum Saalbalkon /
Bridge towards auditorium balcony

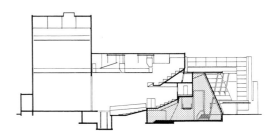

Foyer mit Garderobe /
Foyer with coat-check

Saal / Auditorium

Detail Treppenaufgang /
Detail stairs

Wohnkomplex
Düren, Deutschland, 1993–1997

Das Baugelände liegt auf einem wenig attraktiven Stadtgebiet. Statt sich an den vorgegebenen Richtplan zu halten, der eine Verteilung der einzelnen Blocks über das ganze Gelände vorsah, entschied sich Hertzberger für eine zeilenförmige Anordnung entlang der Baugrenze und damit für eine Hofrandbebauung. Der Hof ist von allen Seiten zugänglich, und die Hofmitte wird von einer Straße durchquert. Die durchlaufende Dachfläche sowie die Plattenverkleidung, die die unterschiedlichen Bauhöhen sichtbar macht, schaffen ein einheitliches Bild. Alle Wohnungen sind von der Hofseite erschlossen und können je nach Haustyp über das Treppenhaus oder über die verschiedenen Galerien erreicht werden.

Housing Complex
Düren, Germany, 1993–1997

The building site is located in a rather dismal part of town. Instead of keeping to the prescribed extension plan and distributing the building blocks all over the site, Hertzberger arranged them in a line along the perimeter thus creating a square building block around a court. This court is accessible from all sides and a street runs over it in the middle. The continuous roof and the plinth, which shows the difference in building height, unify the whole complex. All dwellings have their entry on the court side and, depending on the housing typology, can be reached directly by stairs or over the different galleries.

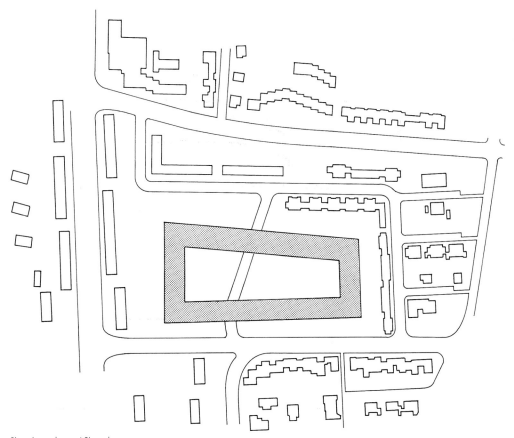

Situationsschema / Site scheme

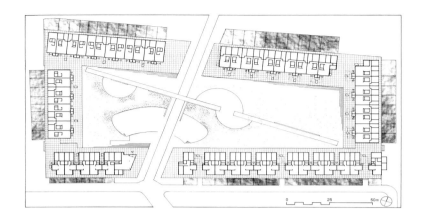

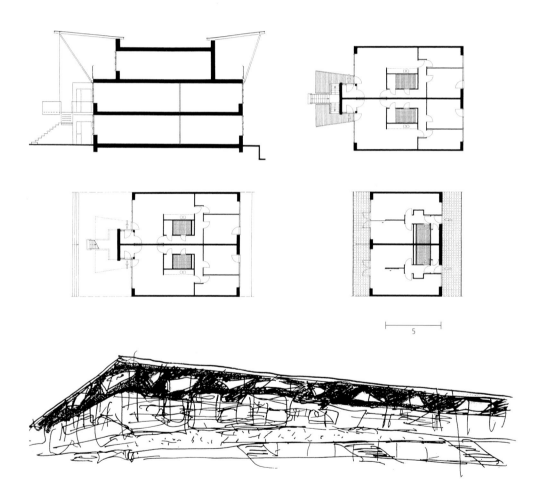

Grundriß Erdgeschoß / Ground floor plan
Schnitt und Grundrißbeispiele / Section and ground plan examples
Entwurfsskizze / Design sketch

Balkone / Balconies
Gemeinschaftlicher Innenhof / Communal courtyard

Balkontypen / Balcony types

Ansicht Südfassade / View of south facade

Masterplan Rummelsburger Bucht, Stralauer Halbinsel
Berlin, 1992–

Charakteristisch für den Entwurf sind die Häuserreihen, die perpendikular zum Wasser hin orientiert sind. Die ursprünglich vorgesehenen Kanäle wurden durch «Grünkanäle» ersetzt. Diese Struktur ermöglicht eine visuelle Öffnung in Richtung beider Ufer. Drei Fabrikschornsteine blieben als Erinnerung an die frühere Nutzung des Gebiets erhalten. Für den westlichen Teil der Halbinsel wurden halboffene Blockbauten vorgesehen, um die bestehenden Wohngebäude und die historischen Industrieanlagen so natürlich wie möglich zu integrieren. Quer durch das Gebiet läuft ein Fußweg. Zwei der Blocks hat Hertzberger selbst entworfen: einen langgestreckten Wohnblock, der quer über die Straße geführt ist, und einen zweiten in der Nordostecke der Halbinsel, dessen gekrümmter Teil den Ausblick auf's Wasser gestattet.

Rummelsburger Bucht, Stralauer Halbinsel. Masterplan
Berlin, Germany, 1992–

Characteristic of the plan are the building rows that are perpendicularly oriented towards the waterfront. The canals which were initially proposed have been transformed into green "canals". This structure guarantees a visual openness in the direction of both watersides. Three factory chimneys have been maintained as monuments of the former use of the area. In the western part of the area, half-closed building blocks have been introduced in order to integrate the existing housing and the historical industrial buildings as naturally as possible. Diagonally, a walkway runs through the area. Hertzberger designed two blocks himself: a long stretched building block which crosses the road and one in the north-east corner of which the curved part offers a view towards the water.

Perspektivische Skizze des bebauten Gebiets /
Sketch in perspective of the builtup area

Modell / Model

a. Bestand / Existing buildings
b. Zu erhaltender Bestand / Buildings to be preserved
c. Konzept / Concept
d. Überlagerung / Superimposition
e. Sichtlinien / View lines
f. Städtebaulicher Entwurf / Masterplan
g. Städtebauliche Situuierung der Plätze / Urban structuring of squares
h. Grünzonen / Main green elements

Perspektivische Skizze
und Grundriß Block A /
Perspective sketch
and plan of block A

Modell und Grundriß
Block B /
Model and ground plan
of block B

Situationsschema /
Site scheme

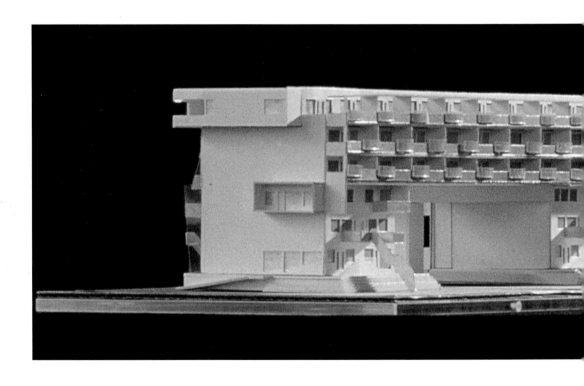

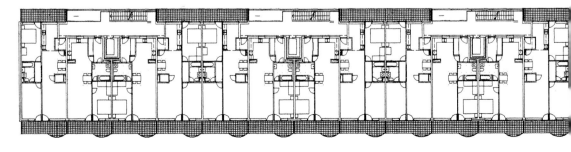

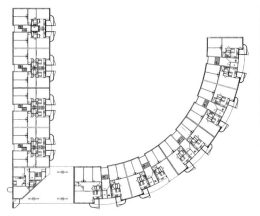
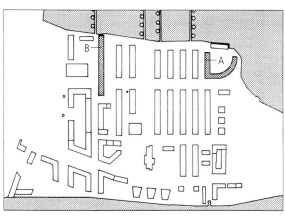

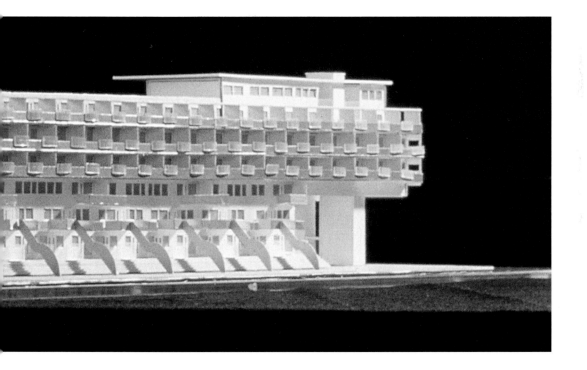

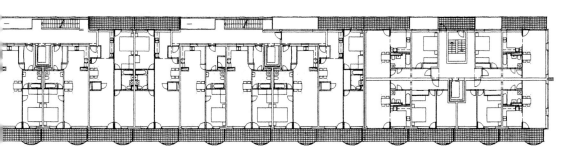

Gebaute Landschaft. Industriegelände

Wettbewerb, 1. Preis, Freising, Deutschland, 1993

Built Landscape. Business Area

Competition, first prize, Freising, Germany, 1993

Immer schneller wuchern die Städte in die Landschaft hinein, zehren sie auf und zerstückeln sie. Statt den natürlichen Raum weiter zu schwächen, wurde hier nun auf dem Baugelände eine künstliche Landschaft geschaffen. Diese «gebaute Landschaft» nimmt die Form von ausgehobenen Reihen an – als Ackerfurchen zu lesen –, die der Landschaft ein markantes Gesicht geben und so die fragwürdige Alternative von «ländlich» und «städtisch» unterlaufen sollen. In diesen «Furchen» können verschiedenartige Gebäude in beliebiger Zusammenstellung gebaut werden, vorausgesetzt, daß die Höhe der welligen, begrünten Dachstreifen nicht überschritten wird. Die offenen Bereiche zwischen den Reihen fungieren abwechselnd als Straßen und Grünzonen. Eine zentrale Fußgängerstraße stanzt eine Abfolge von Durchgängen in die gebauten Zeilen. An diesen Durchgängen und auf dem dreieckigen Platz liegen öffentliche Gebäude und städtische Einrichtungen.

The city is devouring the landscape at a rapid pace and in a much too piecemeal fashion. Rather than impair the landscape further, an artificial landscape has been assembled on the site. This "gebaute Landschaft" is dug into rows to give a striking pattern to the landscape, thus avoiding the questionable alternative of "urban" and "rural". In the ploughs can be built a variety of accommodations in a chosen configuration, provided that the curved greenery-clad strips of roof are adhered to as the upper limit. In between the rows are open zones, alternating streets and green space. A central pedestrian street punches a succession of gateways through the built rows. Public and urban facilities are located at these gateways and on the triangular square.

Modell / Model

Situationsschema / Site scheme

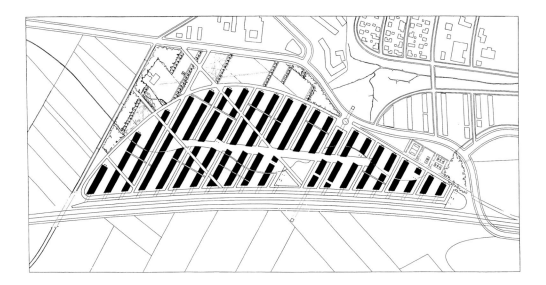

Entwurfsskizze / Design sketch

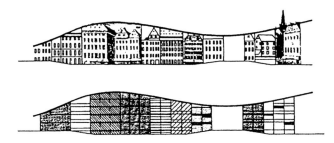

Fassadenschema / Facade scheme

Le Corbusier, Fort l'Empereur, Alger «chaque architecte y fera la villa qu'il lui plaira d'imaginer» (La ville radieuse, 1933, S./p. 247)

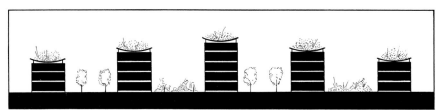

Längsschnittschema / Vertical section scheme

Dachstreifen ordnen die darunterliegende
Vielfalt wie Raster / Grid-like roof
strips give structure to the variety below

Integration in die Landschaft /
Integration into the existing landscape

Ausgestaltungsfreiheit unter den Dächern /
Design freedom beneath the roofs

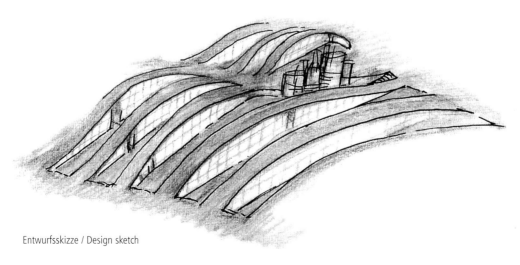

Entwurfsskizze / Design sketch

Auditorium

Wettbewerb, Rom, Italien, 1993

Das Gebäude wurde weniger als isoliertes Objekt denn als teilweise ausgehöhlter, künstlicher Hügel aufgefaßt. Dieser neue Hügel füllt eine Lücke zwischen zwei bereits bestehenden natürlichen Hügeln. Das städtische Straßennetz, das dem Entwurf zugrunde liegt und sich aus dem Axialsystem des Stadtgrundrisses ergibt, setzt sich sozusagen bis unter das weitläufige, dreieckige Dach des Gebäudes fort. Dieses Dach, ein autonomes Gebilde, formt den Hügel in Richtung der Durchgangsstraßen. Es überzieht die drei Konzertsäle sowie die Betriebseinrichtungen. Einschnitte in den Hügel schaffen unterschiedliche Ebenen, durch die während des Tages natürliches Licht einfallen kann und bei Nacht künstliches Licht auf die Stadt zurückstrahlt. Die Besucher gelangen über die zwischen den Sälen gelegenen Treppen ins Foyer hinunter. Zuunterst befinden sich die größeren Buffets. Öffentliche Zonen wie Museum und Bibliothek liegen außerhalb. Das gewellte Dach nimmt dem Projekt den Charakter eines Gebäudes und läßt es wie eine Landschaft wirken.

Auditorium

Competition, Rome, Italy, 1993

The building has been considered not as an isolated object but more as an artificial hill which has been partly excavated. This new hill fills the gap between two existing hills. The urban grid which formed the basis of the plan and which was dictated by the axial system of the city plan runs, as it were, under the huge triangular roof. This roof, an autonomous structure, forms the hill towards the traffic roads. It covers the three concert halls and the service structures. Cuts in the hill form differences in level from which natural light can enter during the day and artificial light reflects on the city at night. The user can descend between the auditoriums to the foyer along a cascade of stairs. The main buffets are to be found at the lowest point. Public areas, such as museum and library, are placed at the exterior. The undulating roof makes the project more of a landscape than a building.

Skizzen / Sketches

Modell / Model

Grundriß / Ground floor plan
1. Eingangshalle / Entrance hall
2. Garderobe / Cloakroom
3. Foyer / Foyer
4. Großes Auditorium / Large auditorium
5. Mittleres Auditorium /
   Medium-size auditorium
6. Kleines Auditorium / Small auditorium

Entwurfsskizze / Design sketch

Schnitt / Section

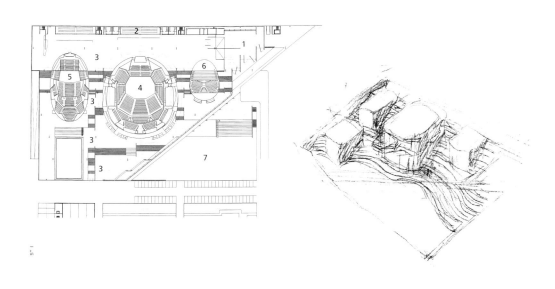

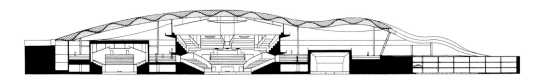

Siedlung Veerse Poort. Masterplan
Middelburg, 1995–

Das neue Wohngebiet hat ländlichen Charakter: die Landschaft wird bis in den Stadtkern hinein spürbar. Es besteht
aus freistehenden Doppelwohnhäusern sowie sieben weiteren urbanen Kerneinheiten, die wie nach außen ge-
wendete städtische Wohnblocks wirken. Die Häuser
schließen öffentliche Plätze ein, während die Gärten sich
nach außen orientieren. Die Plätze sind von einer Ring-
straße aus für den Verkehr erschlossen. Die Umgebung
jenseits der Wohngebiete ist als Park gestaltet und nur für
Fußgänger zugänglich. Im Zentrum liegt eine langge-
streckte Wasserzone.

Veerse Poort Residential Area. Masterplan
Middelburg, 1995–

The new neighbourhood has a rural character: the landscape can be felt to the city core. It consists of double
freestanding houses and seven more urban nuclei which
are like city blocks turned inside out. The gardens have
been oriented towards the outside and the buildings sur-
round public squares. Traffic can reach these squares from
the ring road. Beyond these residential precincts, the area,
conceived as a park is only accessible to pedestrians. A
long strech of water is centrally placed.

a

b

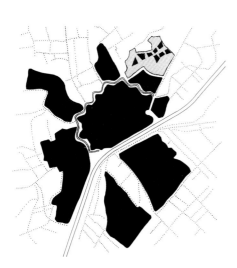

Lageplan Middelburg / Middelburg location plan

c

a. Traditioneller Wohnblock / Traditional housing block
b. Das Innere nach außen gekehrt / The inside turned out
c. Ohne Straßenzwang / Without street constraints

Masterplan für die Ausführung /
Execution masterplan

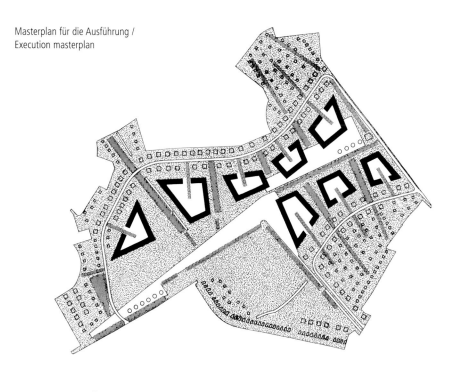

Fahrradverkehr / Bicycle paths

Fußgänger / Pedestrians

Autoverkehr / Car traffic

Entwurfsskizze /
Design sketch

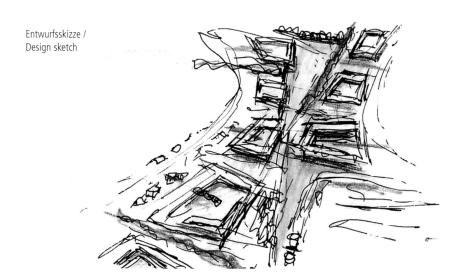

Brandenburger Landtag. Bürogebäude
Wettbewerb, Potsdam, Deutschland, 1995

Landtag Brandenburg Office Building
Competition, Potsdam, Germany, 1995

Das Gebäude wurde nicht als autonomes Objekt entworfen, sondern teilweise unterirdisch angelegt. Was als «Gebäude» erscheint, sind nur Teile des Ganzen. Der Baukörper ist in den grünen Abhang eingegliedert. An der Ufer- und an der Eingangsseite drückt sich das Gebäude selbst klar aus. Dort ist seine allgemeine Bedeutung explizit gemacht. Die drei parallel zum Wasser angeordneten Flügel sind durch ein senkrecht unterhalb der Flügel verlaufendes Foyer verbunden, das den Blick auf's Wasser und auf's Stadtzentrum erlaubt.

The building has not been conceived as an autonomous object, but has been placed partially under the ground. Only certain building parts manifest themselves as "buildings". The building has been subordinated to the green slope. On the waterfront and the entrance side the building expresses itself clearly. There, the general importance of the building is explicit. The three wings, parallel to the water, are connected by a perpendicular hall which is placed underneath the wings and permits a view on the water and on the city center.

«Betonlandschaft» des PCF-Gebäudes in Paris von Oscar Niemeyer, 1967 /
"Concrete landscape" of the PCF building in Paris by Oscar Niemeyer, 1967

Situationsschema / Site scheme

Grundriß Erdgeschoß und erstes Obergeschoß /
Ground and 1st floor plan
1. Eingang / Entrance
2. Zentraler Raum / Central space
3. Büro / Office
5. Plenarsaal / Assembly hall
6. Bibliothek / Library
7. Luftraum / Air space

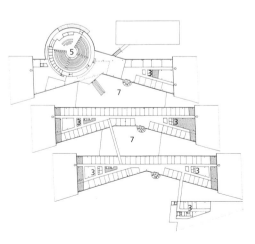

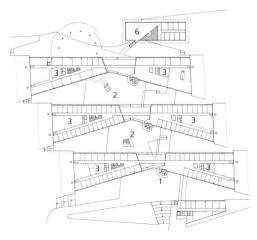

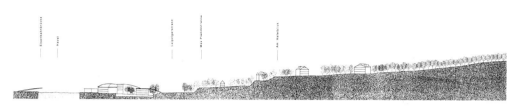

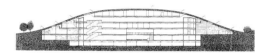

Perspektivische Skizze / Sketch in perspective

Schnitt / Section

Modell / Model

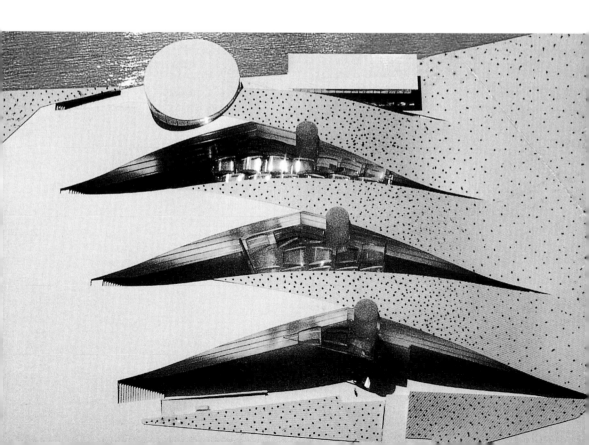

Musicon
Wettbewerb, Bremen, Deutschland, 1995

Der Gebäude ist als autonomer Baukörper entworfen. Auf einer Vielzahl dünner Pilotis ruhend, scheint es über der Umgebung zu schweben und gibt so für Passanten den Blick in den Park frei. Zwischen dem unteren Gebäude und der darüber schwebenden Schale besteht keine Verbindung. Das Musicon wird nur von den Eingängen und Ausgängen, den Aufzügen, Treppen und Pilotis getragen. Der darunterliegende Raum ist vielfach nutzbar. Dort können Märkte, Konzerte oder andere Veranstaltungen abgehalten werden. In sich als introspektives Gebäude gestaltet, bietet das Musicon durch ein Horizontalfenster im Foyer sowie durch das «Fenster zur Stadt», das sich über die Höhe von drei Stockwerken zieht, einen königlichen Ausblick. Abends, wenn das Foyer erleuchtet ist, haben die Passanten Einblick in das Innenleben des Gebäudes.

Musicon
Competition, Bremen, Germany, 1995

The building has been conceived as an autonomous building block. It rests on a large quantity of thin "pilotis" and thus seems to float above the surroundings. This permits a view of the park to the passers-by. There is no connection between the lower building and the floating dish above. Only the entrances and exits, the elevators, stairs, and the pilotis hold the Musicon up. The space underneath can be used in many ways; for market purposes, concerts and other social events. In itself, the Musicon is an introspective building. Through the horizontal window in the foyer and "the window towards the town", which is three storeys high, one has a royal view of the city. At night when the foyer is illuminated the passers-by have a view of the inner life of the building.

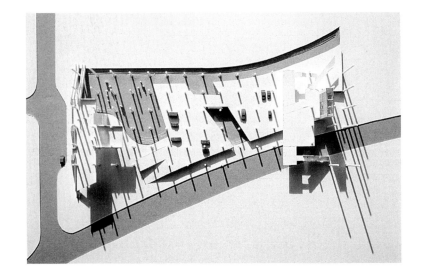

Situationsschema /
Site scheme

Modell / Model

Schnitt / Section

Entwurfsskizze /
Design sketch

192

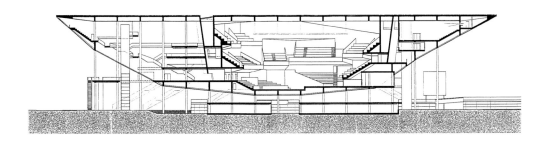

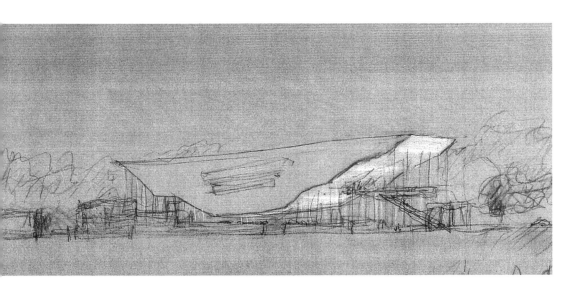

Luxor-Theater
Wettbewerb, Rotterdam, 1996

Luxor Theater
Competition, Rotterdam, 1996

Das Ausgangskonzept war eine kubische Hülle, besser gesagt, eine schützende Box, die Bühnenturm und Zuschauersaal mitsamt dem anschließenden Foyer und den Betriebsräumen so einschließen sollte, daß die spezifischen Formen nicht nach außen hervortraten. Im Sinne einer plastischen Wirkung wurde die «Verpackung» indes an einigen Stellen entfernt und der Inhalt sichtbar gemacht. Das Theater wurde leicht erhöht, um das freie Erdgeschoß für andere städtische Einrichtungen frei zu halten, wie sie sich gerne in Theaternähe ansiedeln. Das Foyer erhält durch Balkone und Treppen deutliche Akzente. Die hohe, kubische Form macht den Bau zu einem Signal im Rotterdamer Hafen.

The basic concept was to make a cubic envelope, or better, a protective box, in which the flytower and the auditorium, surrounded by the foyer and service rooms, would be put in such a manner that their specific form would not appear on the outside. In a plastic sense, the "packing" has been eliminated in certain spots in order to let the contents transpire to the outside. The theater has been elevated in order to keep the ground free for other urban facilities which are attracted by the theater itself. The foyer has been strongly articulated with stairs and balconies. The high cubic form makes it into a beacon along the Rotterdam Harbor.

Jorge de Oteiza «Caja Metafisica» (1958).
Nationalmuseum, Kunstzentrum Königin Sofia, Madrid. /
National Museum, Art Center Queen Sofia, Madrid.

Grundrisse, Ansichten, Querschnitte /
Ground plans, elevations, sections
1. Freiraum für Läden / Free space for shops
2. Eingang / Entrance
3. Foyer / Foyer
4. Saal / Hall

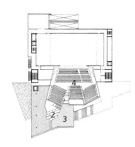

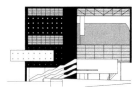

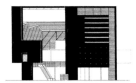

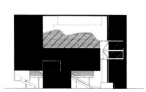

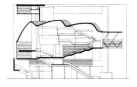

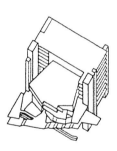

Modell / Model

«Inhalt» und «Verpackung»/
"Content" and "packaging"

Perspektivische Skizze des Foyers /
Sketch of the foyer in perspective

Axel-Springer-Multimedienzentrum.
Städtebauprojekt
Wettbewerb, Berlin, 1996

Axel Springer Multi-Media Center.
Urban Design Project
Competition, Berlin, Germany, 1996

Die Blockbauten akzentuieren die Ausrichtung der benachbarten Wohnblocks und geben ihnen eine neue Form. Im Originalplan stehen Block 1 und 2 erhöht, so daß die Straße bis in die Höfe geführt werden kann. Der traditionelle, geschlossene Innenhofcharakter ist dadurch vermieden. Block 3, der interessanteste Teil des Komplexes, ist an die Baulinie gesetzt, während das Blockzentrum als Park konzipiert wurde, der von drei Seiten zugänglich ist. Die oszillierenden Gebäudestreifen um den Park herum mit zurückgesetzten Obergeschossen sollen Wohnungen aufnehmen, die übrigen Teile Büro- und Gewerberäumlichkeiten.

The building blocks accentuate the directions of the surrounding blocks and transform these into a new form. In the original plans the blocks 1 and 2 are lifted so that the street can penetrate under them into the courts. The traditional closed court character has been avoided. Block 3, the most interesting one, follows, on the perimeter, the building lines, whereas the core of the block has been conceived as a public park accessible from three directions. Around the park, the oscillating buildingbands with set back upper storeys are destined for housing. The other parts contain offices and commercial spaces.

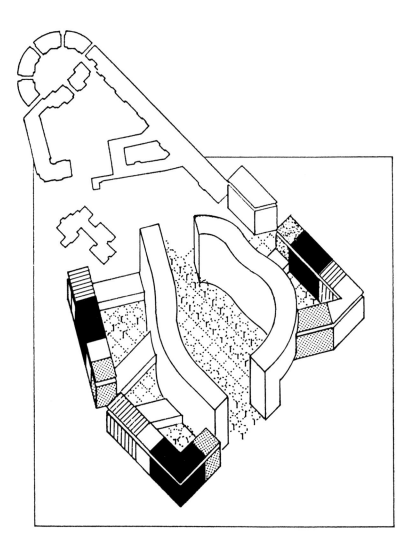

Axonometrieschema /
Axonometric scheme

Perspektivische Skizze /
Sketch in perspective

Querschnitt / Cross section

Modellausschnitt /
Part of the model

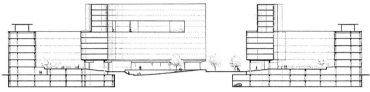

Peninsula. Städtebauprojekt

Tel Aviv, Israel 1996–

Der Entwurf ist als Fortsetzung des städtebaulichen Programms von Patrick Geddes konzipiert. Die vorhandenen Hauptstraßen wurden erweitert und die Siedlungsquadranten, die durch das Raster entstehen, sind mit Grünzonen und Sackgassen durchsetzt. Der alte Hafen mit dem Kran bleibt als historisches Denkmal erhalten, die umliegende Gegend wird als Erholungsgebiet genutzt. An dieses Gebiet schließt sich ein langgezogener Park an, in dem kulturelle Einrichtungen untergebracht werden können. Die zum Meer hin liegende Seite der Halbinsel ist mit Wohnpiers auf hohen Säulen geplant, während auf der zum Fluß gekehrten Seite verschiedene Wohntürme vorgesehen sind. Obwohl der Entwurf der architektonischen Interpretation genügend Freiraum bietet, liegt dem Gebäudetypus die städtische Villa zugrunde, und er gleicht darin der «weißen Stadt» Tel Avivs.

Urban Design Peninsula

Competition, Tel Aviv, Israel, 1996–

The plan is conceived as a continuation of the urban scheme of Patrick Geddes. The existing main streets have been extended. The residential quadrants formed by the grid have green pockets and dead-end streets. The old port with its crane is preserved as a historic monument. The surrounding area is used as a recreational zone. Connected to this zone is a long elongated strip of park where cultural buildings can be accommodated. On the sea side, the plan has residential piers on high columns; on the river side, residential towers have been projected. Although the plan leaves much room for architectonic interpretation, the housing type is based on the urban villa, similar to that of the "white city" of Tel Aviv.

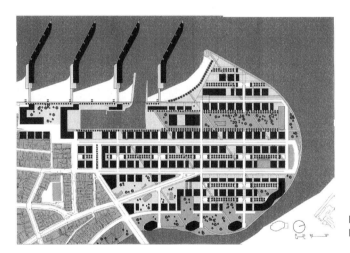

Bebauungsplan /
Masterplan

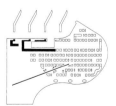 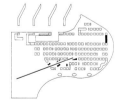

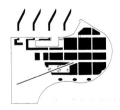 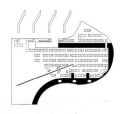

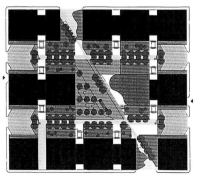

Siedlungsquadrant / Residental quadrant

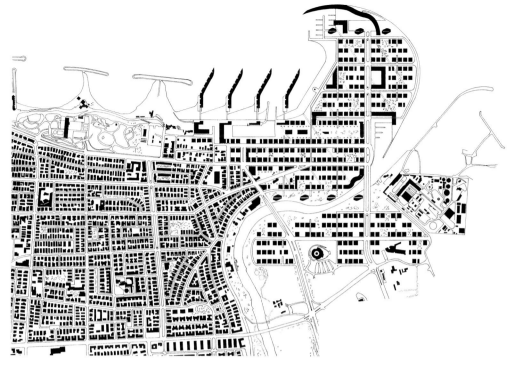

Bebauungsplan mit möglichen Erweiterungen und Anbindungen an die Stadt /
Masterplan with possible extensions and links to the city

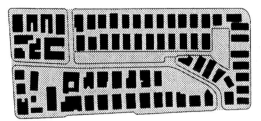

Existing Geddes urban structure

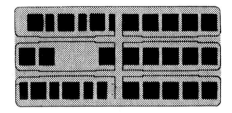

Proposed new urban structure

Skizze des alten Hafenbereichs / Sketch of the existing harbor area

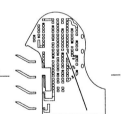

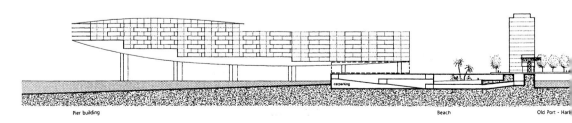

Pier building   Beach   Old Port - Harb

Querschnitt / Cross section

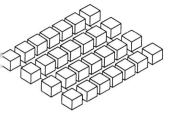
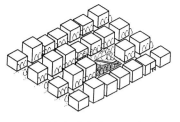
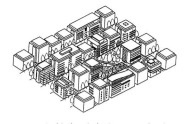

Städtebauliche Struktur /
Urban structure

Städtebauliche Interpretation /
Urban interpretation

Architektonische Interpretation /
Architectural interpretation

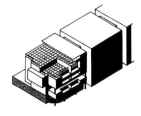

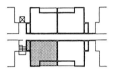
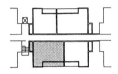
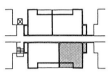

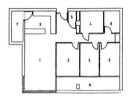
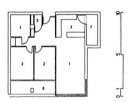

Wohnungstypen /
Apartment types

1. Wohnzimmer / Living room
2. Schlafzimmer / Bedroom
3. Küche / Kitchen
4. Badezimmer / Bathroom
5. Toiletten / Restrooms
6. Abstellraum / Storage room
7. Schutzraum / Shelter
8. Loggia / Loggia

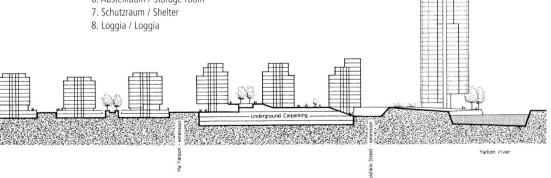

Biographie / Biography

Born in Amsterdam, 6 July 1932

Studied at the Technical University of Delft, graduated in 1958 with Prof. M. Duintjer

Own office since 1958

Editor of FORUM (Dutch magazine), with Aldo van Eyck, Jaap Bakema and others, 1959–63

Teacher at the Academy of Architecture, Amsterdam, 1965–69

Professor at the Technical University of Delft since 1970

Honorary member of the Académie Royale de Belgique since 1975

Visiting professor at several American and Canadian universities: 1966–81, 1987, 1993

Visiting professor at the University of Geneva (Switzerland), 1982–86

Honorary Member of the Bund Deutscher Architekten since 1983

Professor at the University of Geneva (Switzerland), 1986–93

Chairman of the Berlage Institute Amsterdam, 1990–95

Knight of the Order of Oranje Nassau, 1991

Honorary Fellow of the Royal Institute of British Architects since 1991

Honorary Member of the Akademie der Künste Berlin (art academy) since 1993

Detail Markant-Theater, siehe S. 167 oben / Markant Theater, detail, see p. 167 top

Projektverzeichnis/List of Projects

1955   Community unit, Vlaardingen
        (together with T. Hazewinkel)*;
        Neighborhood Center, Amsterdam
        (together with J. Meyer and C. Kneulman,
        competition, first prize)*
1959   Students' house (1966), Weesperstraat
        7–57, Amsterdam (together with
        T. Hazewinkel and H.A. Dicke)
1960   Delftse Montessori school (1966),
        Jacoba van Beierenlaan 166, Delft
1962   Factory extension "LinMij" (1964), Molen-
        werf 2, Amsterdam (demolished in 1995)
1964   Church, Driebergen (competition)*;
        Residential building for elderly and dis-
        abled people "De Drie Hoven" (1974),
        Louis Bouwmeesterstraat 377, Amsterdam
1966   Town hall, Valkenswaard (competition)*
1967   House conversion (1967), Laren;
        Town hall, Amsterdam (competition)*
1968   Houses type Monogoon*; Extension
        Delftse Montessori School (1970), Delft;
        Office building "Centraal Beheer" (1972)
        (together with Lucas & Niemeijer), Prins
        Willem Alexanderlaan 651, Apeldoorn
1969   Housing Diagoon (1970), Gebbenlaan,
        Delft; Townplanning city extension (1973),
        Deventer*
1970   Townplanning Nieuwmarkt,
        Amsterdam (competition)*
1971   Memorandum of objectives and criteria
        for renewal of city center (1972),
        with De Boer, Lambooij, Goudappel and
        others, Groningen
1972   Neighborhood center "De Schalm" (1974),
        Dreef 1, Deventer
1973   Music Center "Vredenburg" (1978),
        Vredenburgpassage 77, Utrecht
1974   City Center plan, with Van den Broek
        and Bakema, Eindhoven*; Townplanning
        consultant for the University, Groningen,
        Proposal for a university library, Gronin-
        gen*

1975   Houses, shops and parking near Musis
        Sacrum and renewal of the Theater Musis
        Sacrum, Arnhem*
1976   Institute for Ecological Research, Heteren*
1977   2nd extension Delftse Montessori School
        (1981), Delft; Townplanning Schouwburg-
        plein, Rotterdam*
1978   40 houses (1980), Westbroek; Urban
        renewal "Haarlemmer Houttuinen"
        (1982), Nieuwe Houttuinen, Amsterdam;
        Library, Loenen aan de Vecht*
1979   Housing project "Kassel-Dönche"
        (1982), Heinrich-Schütz-Allee, Kassel
        (West Germany); Office building "Ministry
        of Social Welfare and Employment" (1990),
        Anna van Hannoverstraat 4, The Hague;
        Extension to "LinMij", Amsterdam*
1980   Design of pavilions, bus stops and market
        facilities for the "Vredenburg" Square
        (1982), Utrecht; "Apollo Schools"
        (1983) – Amsterdamse Montessori School,
        Willem Witsenstraat 14 and Willemspark
        School, Willem Witsenstraat 12, Amster-
        dam; Residential building for the elderly
        "De Overloop" (1984), Boogstraat 1,
        Almere; Building on Forum area, The
        Hague*; Townplanning Römerberg, Frank-
        furt a.M., Germany (competition)*; Hous-
        ing project, Berlin-Spandau, Germany*
1982   Residential building "LiMa" (1986),
        Lindenstrasse 82–84/Markgrafenstrasse
        5–8, Berlin, Germany; "Crèche", Berlin,
        Germany (competition)*
1983   Townplanning Cologne/Mülheim-Nord,
        Germany (competition)*; Office building
        Friedrich-Ebert-Stiftung, Bonn, Germany
        (competition)*; Office building Gruner &
        Jahr, Hamburg, Germany (competition)*
1984   Kindergarten/school
        "De Evenaar" (1986), Ambonplein 59,
        Amsterdam; Extension Academy for the
        Arts "Sint Joost", Breda*

1985	Office building Stadtwerke, Frankfurt a.M., Germany (competition)*; Film Center (academy, museum, library), Berlin, Germany (competition, first prize)*; Extension Town hall, Saint Denis, France (competition)*
1986	Residential buildings "Het Gein" (406 houses and 52 apartments) in Schothorst (opposite the Amersfoort-Schothorst railway station) (1989), Amersfoort; Theater Center Spui (1993), The Hague, building block with: apartments and shops at the Amsterdamse Veerkade and above the Spui, Theater, Spui 187, "Cinematheek" (movie Center), Spui 191, video Center, Spui 189, art Center, Spui 193; Experimental housing project "Zuiderpolder" (floating waterhouses), Haarlem; Townplanning Bicocca-Pirelli, Milan, Italy (competition)*; Museum for painting (Gemäldegalerie), Berlin, Germany (competition)*; Film Center Esplanade, Germany*
1988	Extension for 8 classes and conversion of kindergarten/primary school "Schoolvereniging Aerdenhout Bentveld" (1989), Mr. Enschedéweg 22, Aerdenhout; Residential buildings Amsterdam neigbourhood of 43 units (1996), Haarlem; Residential project Koningscarré, Haarlem*; Residential building, Maastricht (competition)*; Office building Schering, Berlin, Germany (competition)*
1989	Private house/studio 2000, 16 houses in the Muziekwijk-area (near the Almere-Muziekwijk railway station), for the "NWR BouwRAI 90" (1990), Wessel Ilckenstraat 2–32 (even numbers), Almere; "Kijck over den Dijck" residential area Merwestein Noord, Dordrecht; Urban design residential area "Jekerkwartier", Maastricht*; Urban design "Maagjesbolwerk", Zwolle*; French national library building "Bibliothèque de France", Paris, France (competition)*; Cultural Center with concert hall "Kulturzentrum am See", Luzern, Switzerland (competition)*; Street furniture for riverside walk, Rotterdam (competition)*
1990	"Polygoon", kindergarten/school with 16 classrooms (for the "NWRBouwRAI 92")

(1992), Hollywoodlaan 109, Almere; 11 semi-detached houses (for the "NWR BouwRAI 92") (1992), James Stewartstraat (between Ingrid Bergmanstraat and Bette Davisstraat), Almere; Office building "Benelux Merkenbureau" (1993), Bordewijklaan 15, Den Haag (tel.: 070-3491111); Extension to "Centraal Beheer" office building (1995), Prins Willem Alexanderlaan 651, Apeldoorn; Study of extension to Vredenburg Music Center involving 3rd auditorium and a matching urban design for the Utrecht City Project, Utrecht; MediaPark building with housing, studios and offices, Cologne, Germany (competition, first prize); Agency for the "Nederlandse Bank", Wassenaar (competition)*; Urban design for a suburb, Grenoble, France (competition)*

1991	Extension Willemspark School (1993), Amsterdam; Library and "De Nieuwe Veste" – Center for Art and Music (Music and Dance department) (1993), Molenstraat 6, Breda; Urban design "Noordendijk", Dordrecht; YKK Dormitory and guest house, Kurobe, Japan; Office building in the Richti-Areal, Zürich-Wallisellen, Switzerland (competition)*; City Theater, Delft (competition)*; School Collège Anatole France, Drancy, France (competition)*
1992	Chassé Theater (1995), Claudius Prinsenlaan 8, Breda; Music Center Amsterdam, Amsterdam*; Office project Sony-Potsdamerplatz, Berlin, Germany (competition)*; Berlin Olympia 2000: urban townplanning "Rummelsburger Bucht", Berlin, Germany (competition, first prize);
1993	Kindergarten/school "Anne Frank" (1994), Rozenstraat 36, Papendrecht; LOM-school "De Bombardon" (school for children with learning or educational difficulties) (1995), Simon van Collemstraat 7, Almere; Residential area (1996), Vrijheer van Eslaan, Rozenstraat, Goudenregenstraat (31 residences), Papendrecht; Theater Markant (1996), Markt 32, Uden; Housing complex with 136 units (1996), Rotterdamer Straße, Düren, Germany (competition, first prize); Residential buildings Stralauer Halbinsel Block 7 and 8, Berlin, Germany; Urban design and masterplan Stralauer

Halbinsel, Berlin, Germany; Montessori College Oost, school for 1600 students, Amsterdam; Urban design for the Clemenänger area, Freising, Germany (competition, first prize); Extension Vanderveen Department Store (1997), Koopmansplein, Assen; Study of design for a new academy for arts, Rotterdam*; Residential building Witteneiland, Amsterdam (competition)*; Auditorium, Rome, Italy (competition)*

1994   Extension to the library (1996), Molenstraat 6, Breda; Bijlmermonument, in cooperation with Georges Descombes, Amsterdam; Governmental office building Ceramique area, Maastricht

1995   Residential buildings Stralauer Halbinsel Block 12, Berlin, Germany; Urban design residential area Veerse Poort, Middelburg; Primary School, Venlo; Residential buildings Prooyenspark, Middelburg; Extension Fire Department School, Schaarsbergen (competition)*; Office building "Landtag Brandenburg", Potsdam, Germany (competition)*; Music Theater "Musicon", Bremen, Germany (competition)*; Luxor Theater, Rotterdam (competition)*; Urban design railroad surroundings Tiburtina/Tuscolana, Rome, Italy (competition)*; Primary school, Venlo

1996–   Bijlmer monument (in cooperation with Georges Descombes), second stage, Amsterdam; Kindergarten and primary Montessori school "De Eilanden", Amsterdam; Urban design village Center, Dallgow, Germany (competition, first prize); "Paradijssel" residential area, Cappelle aan de IJssel; Urban design Peninsula, Tel Aviv, Israel (competition, first prize); Urban design Axel Springer Multimedia, Berlin, Germany (competition)*; House on Borneo Island, Amsterdam; Extension to residential building "De Overloop", Almere Haven; Urban design Theresienhöhe, Munich, Germany (competition)*; Lothar Gunther Buchheim Museum, Feldafing, Germany (competition)*; Academy of Arts and Design, Kolding, Denmark (competition, first prize)*; Ichthus Hogeschool, Rotterdam (competition)*

1997   Theater, Helsingør, Denmark (competition, first prize)

*= not executed

Auszeichnungen / Awards

1968	City of Amsterdam Award for architecture; for the students' housing in Amsterdam
1974	Eternit award; for the office building "Centraal Beheer" in Apeldoorn
1974	Fritz Schumacher award; for entire oeuvre
1980	A.J. van Eck award; for the Vredenburg Music Center in Utrecht
1980	Honorable mention Eternit award; for the "Vredenburg" Music Center in Utrecht
1985	Merkelbach award, city of Amsterdam award for architecture; for the Apollo Schools in Amsterdam
1988	Merkelbach award, city of Amsterdam award for architecture; for the school "De Evenaar" in Amsterdam
1989	Richard Neutra Award for Professional Excellence
1989	Berliner Architekturpreis, city of West Berlin award; for the Lindenstrasse/Markgrafenstrasse housing project in Berlin
1991	Premio Europa Architettura, Fondazione Tetraktis award; for the entire oeuvre
1991	Berlage Flag, Dutch award for architecture; for the Ministry of Social Welfare and Employment in The Hague
1991	BNA (association of Dutch architects) award; for the entire oeuvre
1991	Concrete Award; for the Ministry of Social Welfare and Employment in The Hague
1993	Prix Rhénan 1993, European architecture award for school buildings; for the school "Schoolvereniging Aerdenhout Bentveld" in Aerdenhout

Ausstellungen / Exhibitions

1967   Biennale des Jeunes, Paris (France)
1968   Stedelijk Museum, Amsterdam
1971   Historisch Museum, Amsterdam
1976   Biennale Venice (Italy)
1976   Stichting Wonen, Amsterdam
1980   Kunsthaus, Hamburg (W. Germany)
1985   Berlin (W. Germany)
          Geneva (Switzerland)
          Bordeaux (France)
          Zürich (Switzerland)
          Vienna (Austria)
          Zagreb (Yugoslavia)
          Split (Yugoslavia)
          Braunschweig (W. Germany)
          Hannover (W. Germany)
          Frankfurt (W. Germany)
          Dortmund (W. Germany) and further on.
1985   Stichting Wonen, Amsterdam
1985   Frans Halsmuseum, Haarlem
1986   Fondation Cartier, Jouy-en-Josas (France)
1986   Center Pompidou, Paris (France)
1986   Triennale, Milan (Italy)
1986   Stichting Wonen, Amsterdam
          Montreal (Canada)
          Toronto (Canada)
          Los Angeles (USA)
          Raleigh (USA)
          Blacksburg (USA)
          Philadelphia (USA)
          Tokyo (Japan)
          London (UK)
          Edinburgh (UK) and further
1987   M.I.T., Cambridge (USA)
          and various other universities in the USA
1987   Stichting Wonen, Amsterdam
1988   New York State Council of the Arts, New York (USA)
1989   Global Architecture International, Tokyo (Japan)
1989   Institut Français d'Architecture, Paris (France)

1991   Global Architecture International, Tokyo (Japan)
1991   L'Aquila, Tetraktis, (traveling) exhibition of several projects and travel-sketches of Herman Hertzberger, L'Aguila, (Italy)
1992   World Architecture Triennale, Nara (Japan)
1993   De Beyerd, Breda
1995   Architekturgalerie, Munich (Germany) Centraal Beheer Apeldoorn, De Pronkkamer, Uden, (traveling) exhibition
1995   De Beyerd, Breda
1996   Deutsches Architektur-Museum, Frankfurt a.M.
1997   The Netherlands Architecture Institute, Rotterdam

Veröffentlichungen / Publications

Students' house, Amsterdam
Bouw, 1964, no. 40; Bouwkundig Weekblad, 1966, no. 24; Goed Wonen, 1966, no. 9; Domus, September 1967; World Architecture, 1967, no. 4; Architecture, Forms, Functions, 1968; Baumeister, 1968, no. 8; A+U, 1977, no. 75; L'Architecture d'Aujourd'hui, 1968, no. 137; Werk, 1968, no. 5

Montessori school, Delft
Bouw, 1969, no. 8; Bouwkundig Weekblad, 1968, no. 9; Goed Wonen, 1967, no. 8; The Architectural Review, 1975, no. 936; La Maison, 1968, no. 6; L'Architecture d'Aujourd'hui, 1968; Harvard Educational Review, 1969, no. 4; Baumeister, June 1969; Bâtiment, 1977, no. 70; A+U, 1977, no. 75; Architecture in Greece, 1979, no. 13

Factory extension LinMij, Amsterdam
Bouwkundig Weekblad, 1966, no. 4; World Architecture, 1966, no. 3; L'Architecture d'Aujourd'hui, "Industrie", 1967; A+U, 1977, no. 75; Werk, 1966, no. 11

Church, Driebergen
Bouwkundig Weekblad, 1964, 165-171; A+U, 1977, no. 75

Residential building for elderly and disabled people "De Drie Hoven", Amsterdam
de Architect, 1975, no. 4; Bouw, 1976, no. 12; Polytechnisch Tijdschrift, 1975, no. 17; Bauen + Wohnen, 1976, no. 1; Baumeister, 1976, no. 2; The Architectural Review, 1976, no. 948; Das Altenheim, April 1976; Lotus International, 1976, no. 11; Kunst und Kirche, 1976, no. 2; Arquitecturas, 1976, no. 11; A+U, 1977, no. 75; Domus, 1977, no. 569; Architecture in Greece, 1979, no. 13; Parametro, 1980, no. 88/89

Town hall, Valkenswaard
TABK, 1967, no. 5; Bouwkundig Weekblad, 1967, no. 20; Bauen und Wohnen, 1967, no. 11; Baumeister, 1969, no. 3; A+U, 1977, no. 75

Town hall, Amsterdam
TABK, 1969, no. 1; Forum, extra issue, May 1969; A+U, 1977, no. 75

"Diagoon" housing, Delft
Bouw, 1972, no. 13; Polytechnisch Tijdschrift, 1970, no. 12; TABK, 1970, no. 2; IB systems and components, August 1970; Bauen + Wohnen, 1972, no. 9; Bauwelt, 1976, no. 15; A+U, 1977, no. 75; L'Architecture d'Aujourd'hui, 1978, no. 196

Project Nieuwmarkt, Amsterdam
Forum, November 1970; Plan, 1970, no. 11

Office building "Centraal Beheer", Apeldoorn
Architectuur/Bouwen, 1991, no. 10; Plan, 1970, no. 5; Wonen TABK, 1973, no. 5; Bauwelt, July 1971; L'Architecture d'Aujourd'hui, Dec. 1972/Jan. 1973; Domus, 1973, no. 522/5; Deutsche Bauzeitung, 1973, no. 11; Baumeister, 1973, no. 11; Architectural Design, 1973, no. 2; BP-Kurier, 1974, no. 1; Le Carré Bleu, 1974, no. 2; A+ (architecture, urbanism, design), 1974, no. 81; A+U, 1974, no. 8; Deutsche Bauzeitschrift, August 1974; Architektur Wettbewerbe 79, September 1974; Architecture Plus, September/October 1974; International Lighting Review, 1974, no. 3; Der Spiegel, 1975, no. 10; CREE, 1975, no. 35; TIILI, 1974, no. 2; The Architect's Journal, October 1975; GA Gas + Architecture, 1975, no. 64; Architectural Design, February 1976; Building Design, September 1975; Arquitecturas, 1976, no. 11; Congress, 1977, no. 1; Form, 1977, no. 1; Der Gewerkschafter, March 1977; project-documentation Technical University-Delft, 1971; L'Architecture d'Aujourd'hui, 1981, no. 213; Arnulf Lüchinger, Strukturalismus in Architektur und Städtebau, Stuttgart 1980; A. Colquhoun. Essays in Architectural Criticism: Modern Architecture and Historical Change, Cambridge/London 1981 (published before in Architecture Plus, 1974); Album 2, 1983; Designers Journal, 1985, no. 12; L'architecture d'Aujourd'hui, 1990. no. 272; Office Age, 1991, no. 16; Der Architekt, 1995, no. 5; Casabella, 1995, no. 627; Baumeister, 1996, no. 2

Neighborhood center "De Schalm", Deventer
Bouw, 1972, no. 45; The Architectural Review, 1973, no.
911

Music Center Vredenburg, Utrecht
Bouw, 1981, no. 7; Futura, 1978, no. 12; Wonen TABK,
1979, no. 24; The Architectural Review, 1976, no. 948; The
Architectural Review, 1976, no. 949; L'Architecture d'Aujourd'hui, 1978, no. 198; Bauen + Wohnen, 1979, no. 7/8;
Architectural Record, August 1979; Domus, 1979, no. 601;
Key Notes, 1979/1, no. 9; The Architectural Review, February 1980; A+U, 1980, no. 115; Baumeister, April 1980;
L'Architecture d'Aujourd'hui, April 1980; Spazio e Società,
1980, no. 9; Arkitektur, 1980, no. 8; Betonprisma, 1980,
no. 39; Progressive Architecture, July, 1980; project-documentation Technical University-Delft, Februari 1981; Bauwelt, 1981, no. 9; Deutsche Bauzeitschrift, October 1981;
Muziekcentrum Vredenburg Utrecht, Utrecht, 1995

Town planning Schouwburgplein, Rotterdam
Bouw, 1977, no. 8; Bouw, 1978, no. 15

Housing Haarlemmer Houttuinen, Amsterdam
Bouw, 1983, no. 23; Wonen TABK, 1982, no. 18/19; L'Architecture d'Aujourd'hui, 1983, no. 225; Spazio e Società,
1983, no. 23; The Architectural Review, 1985, no. 1062;
A&V, 1986, no. 7; Mies van der Rohe Award for European
Architecture, London/Laren 1990; Romacentro/Il Recu-
pero Urbano, 1990, no. 11

Housing, Kassel-Dönche
L'Architecture d'Aujourd'hui, 1981, no. 215; Stadt, 1982,
no. 8; L'Architecture d'Aujourd'hui, 1983, no. 225; Spazio
e Società, 1983, no. 23; A+U, 1983, no. 159; Betonprisma, 1984, no. 46; The Architectural Review, 1985, no.
1064

**Ministry of Social Welfare and Employement,
The Hague**
Architectuur/Bouwen, 1991, no. 1; The Architectural Review, 1987, no. 1083; L'Architecture d'Aujourd'hui, 1988,
no. 257; The Architectural Review, 1990, no. 1116; Yearbook 1990–1991 Architecture in The Netherlands, Rotterdam 1991; GA Document, 1991, no. 29; Casabella,
1991, no. 583; Werk, Bauen + Wohnen, 1992, no. 1/2;
Techniques et Architecture, 1992, no. 400; Architektur In-
nenarchitektur Technischer Ausbau, 1992, no. 10; Ecíffo,
1992, no. 18; L'Industria delle Costruzioni, 1993, no . 256;
Projectdocumentation Technical University Delft, 1991,
no. 7; Rijksgebouwen, Ministerie van Sociale Zaken en
Werkgelegenheid, Rotterdam, 1991

**Apollo schools, Amsterdam (Amsterdamse
Montessori School and Willemspark School)**
Bouw, 1984, no. 23; Casabella, 1983, no. 493; A+U, 1983,
no. 159; Forum, 1983, no. 3; L'Architecture d'Aujourd'hui,
1984, no. 232; Werk, Bauen und Wohnen, 1984, no. 5; Architectural Design, 1984, no.11/12; Space Design, 1985,
no. 8; Bauwelt, 1985, no. 23; Bauen in Beton, 1986, no. 1

**Housing for the elderly "De Overloop",
Almere-Haven**
Bouw, 1985, no. 21; Casabella, 1984, no. 508; The Archi-
tectural Review, 1985, no. 1058; Techniques et Architec-
ture, 1985, no. 362; Deutsche Bauzeitung, Nov. 1985; L'-
Architecture d'Aujourd'hui, 1987, no. 251

Housing project, Berlin-Spandau
Neue Heimat, 1980, no. 10

Residential building LiMa, Berlin
Arch+, 1984, no. 74; L'Architecture d'Aujourd'hui, 1984,
no. 235; Architectuur/Bouwen, 1987, no. 1; Deutsche
Bauzeitung, 1987, no. 4; The Architectural Review, 1987,
no. 1082; Baumeister, special IBA-issue, 1987, no. 5; A+U,
special IBA-issue, 1987, no. 5; Zuhause, 1987, no. 10; In-
ternationale Bauausstellung Berlin, Berlin 1987; Global
Architecture, 1988, no. 23; Betonprisma, 1989, no. 56; L'-
Architecture d'Aujourd'hui, 1989, no. 266; L'Architettura Cronache e Storia, 1990, no. 413

Elementary school "De Evenaar", Amsterdam
Domus, 1987, no. 682; The Architectural Review, 1987, no.
1085; Architectuur/Bouwen, 1988, no. 2; Modul, 1988,
no. 3; Bauen in Beton/Bouwen met beton/Construire en
béton, 1988; Deutsche Bauzeitschrift, 1990, no. 1; Detail,
1992, no. 1

Theater Center Spui, The Hague
de Architect, 1993, no. 10; RIBA Journal, March 1994; Arquitectura Viva, 1994, no. 38; Yearbook 1993–1994 Architecture in The Netherlands, Rotterdam, 1994; Architec-
tuur/Bouwen, 1986, no.12

**Experimental housing project Zuiderpolder
(floating Waterhouses), Haarlem**
L'Architecture d'Aujourd'hui, 1988, no. 257; Flying Dutch-
man International, 1989, no. 6

Town planning Bicocca – Pirelli, Milan
Casabella, 1986, no. 524; Pirelli Progretto Bicocca, Milan
1986

Museum for painting (Gemäldegalerie), Berlin
Baumeister, 1987, no. 6; Bauwelt, 1987, no. 7/8; AA Files, 1989, no. 16

Film Center Esplanade (academy-cinema-museum-library), Berlin
L'Architecture d'Aujourd'hui, 1985, no. 242; The Architectural Review, 1985, no. 1065; Casabella, 1985, no. 517; Architektur + Wettbewerbe, 1986, no. 127; Baumeister, 1987, no. 6; Global Architecture, 1989, no. 23

Extension primary school "Schoolvereniging Aerdenhout-Bentveld", Aerdenhout
Architectuur/Bouwen, 1990, no. 1; Mies van der Rohe Pavilion Award for European Architecture, Laren 1992; Yearbook 1989–1990 Architecture in The Netherlands, Rotterdam, 1990; Prix Rhénan d'Architecture, Strasbourg, 1993

Residential building Staarstraat, Maastricht
L'Architecture d'Aujourd'hui, 1988, no. 257

Competition "Bibliothèque de France", Paris
L'Architecture d'Aujourd'hui, 1989, no. 265; Le Moniteur, 1989, no. 4478

Kindergarten/elementary school "Polygoon" (BouwRAI 1992), Almere
Archis, 1993, no. 4; Progressive Architecture, 1993, no. 4; Yearbook 1992–1993 Architecture in The Netherlands , Rotterdam 1993

Office Benelux Merkenbureau, The Hague
L'Industria delle Costruzioni, 1996, no. 293

City Theater, Delft
Architectuur/Bouwen, 1991, no. 8

Chassé Theater, Breda
Domus, 1995, no. 776; Archis, 1996, no. 1; The Architectural Review, 1996, no. 2; Chassé Theater, Rotterdam 1995; Yearbook 1995–1996 Architecture in The Netherlands, Rotterdam, 1996; Bauwelt, 1996, no. 23; L'Industria delle Construzioni, 1997, no. 303

LOM-school "De Bombardon", Almere
de Architect, 1996, no. 9; Bauwelt, 1996, no. 28

Competition Auditorium, Rome
l'Arca, 1995, no. 9

Luxor Theater, Rotterdam
Archis, 1996, no. 4

Municipal Library and "De Nieuwe Veste", center for Art and Music. Breda
Yearbook 1993–1994 Architecture in The Netherlands, Rotterdam, 1994

Kindergarten/school "Anne Frank School", Papendrecht
Yearbook 1994–1995, Architecture in The Netherlands, Rotterdam, 1995, Diseño Interior, 1996, no. 54

Theater Markant, Uden
Diseño Interior, 1996, no. 56, Yearbook 1996–1997 Architecture in The Netherlands, Rotterdam, 1997; Dialogue, architecture + design + culture, 1997, no. 1; Abitare, 1997, no. 362

Articles and books on more than 1 project and/or on Hertzberger and/or interviews
The Architectural Record, July 1968; Bauen + Wohnen, 1974, no. 5; Bauen + Wohnen, 1976, no. 1; Arquitecturas, 1976, no. 11; A+U, 1977, no. 75; L'Architecture d'Aujourd'hui, 1978, no 198; Europe/America; Architettura urbane alternative suburbane, Milan 1978; Dutch Art & Architecture Today, 1979, no. 6; Progressive Architecture, March 1980; Projekt, 1981, no. 247; G.R. Blomeyer/B. Tietze, In Opposition zur Moderne, Braunschweig 1980; Stadt 1982, no. 6; L'Architecture d'Aujourd'hui, 1983, no. 225; A+U, 1983, no. 159; CREE – Architecture Intérieure, Oct./Nov. 1984; The Architectural Review, 1985, no. 1055; Archithese, 1985, no. 2; Herman Hertzberger – Six Architectures Photographiées par Johan van der Keuken, Milan 1985; Techniques & Architecture, 1985, no. 362; The Architectural Review, 1985, no. 1064; Arkkitehti, 1985, no. 6/7; Faces, 1985, no. 0; Archithese, 1986, no. 2; Spazio e Società, 1986, no. 33; Umriß, 1986, no. 2/3 (published before in the Dutch magazine Muziek en Dans, 1986, no. 8); Archis, (reprint in English of the issue on the Hertzberger-exhibition from the Stichting Wonen), 1986, no. 12; Bauwelt, 1987, no. 17/18; The Architectural Review, 1987, no. 1085; Arnulf Lüchinger, Herman Hertzberger, 1959– 86, Bauten und Projekte/Buildings and Projects/Bâtiments et Projets, The Hague 1987; The Architect's Journal, 1987, no. 186; AA Files, 1987, no. 16; The Architect's Journal, 1988, no. 187; Techniques & Architecture, 1988, no. 376; Holland Herald, 1988, special edition, no. 6; L'Architecture d'Aujourd'hui, 1988, no. 257; Romolo Continenza, Architetture de Herman Hertzberger dalla forma alla partecipazione, Rome 1988; Spazio e Società, 1988, no. 43; JA

House, 1989; Architecture Today, 1989, no. 1; A&V monografías de Arquitecture y Vivienda, 1989, no. 19; Werk, Bauen + Wohnen, 1989, no. 10; Casabella, 1990, no. 568; The Architectural Review, 1990, no.1116; Wessel Reinink, Herman Hertzberger, (part of the series "Monographs of Dutch architects"), Rotterdam 1990; Herman Hertzberger/ Premio Europa Architettura 1990–1991, Pescara 1991; Architecture and Urbanism (A&U), special edition, all about the works of Herman Hertzberger from 1959 up to and including 1990, April 1991; Architecture and Urbanism (A&U), 1991, no. 248; Architektur, 1991, no. 6; Architetura Quaderni 5, June 1991; Modul, 1992, no. 5; Architecture/Research/Criticism, 1992, no. 3/4; World Architecture, 1992, no. 17; Contemporary Architect Exhibition, Nara (Japan) 1992; Process Architecture, 1993, no. 112; Deutsche Bauzeitung, 1993, no. 10; Casabella, 1993, no. 605; Archis, 1993, no. 12; De Architect, 1994, no. 2; Citizen Office, Weil am Rhein 1994; Ole Bouman/Roemer van Toorn, The Invisible in Architecture, London 1994; Leonardo, Aug./Sept. 1994; Bryan Lawson, Design in Mind, Oxford 1994; The Architectural Review, 1994, no. 1174; Ricerche Progetto, 1994, no. 4; Bouwen met beton/Construire en béton, 1995; Arquitectura Viva, 1997, no. 5; Dialogue, architecture + design + culture, 1997, no. 1

Articles and books written by Herman Hertzberger

– "Ontwerp voor een gebouw van de B.N.A.", Bouwkundig Weekblad, 1955, no. 18, 215
– "Concours d'Emulation 1955 van de studenten", Bouwkundig Weekblad, 1955, 403
– "Inleiding", Forum, 1960, no. 1
– "Weten en geweten", Forum, 1960/61, no. 2, 46–49
– "Verschraalde helderheid", Forum, 1960/61, no. 4, 143–144
– "Three better possibilities", Forum, 1960/61, no. 5, 193
– "Naar een verticale woonbuurt", Forum, 1960/61, no. 8, 264–273
– "Zorg voor of zorg over de architektuur?", Stedebouw en volkshuisvesting, 1961, 216–218
– "Flexibility and polyvalency", Forum, 1962, no. 3
– "Flexibility and polivalency", Ekistics (summary from Forum, no. 3-1962), April 1963
– "The Permeable Surface of the City", World Architecture, 1964, no. 1,
– Forum, 1965, no. 8
– "Gedachten bij de dood van Le Corbusier", Bouwkundig Weekblad, 1965, no. 20, 366
– "Aldo van Eyck 1966", Goed Wonen, 1966, no. 8, 10–12
– "Form and program are reciprocally evocative" and "Identity", Forum, 1967, no. 7
– "Some notes on two works by Schindler", Domus, 1967, no. 454, 2–7 (reprinted in catalogue of the Schindler exhibition, Stedelijk Museum in April 1969), September 1967
– "Place, Choice and Identity", World Architecture, 1967, no. 4, 73–74
– "Form und Programm rufen sich gegenseitig auf", Werk, 1968, no. 3, 200–201
– "Montessori primary school in Delft", Harvard Educational Review: Architecture and Education, vol. 39, no. 4, 1969
– "(Schoonheidscommissies)", Forum, Juli 1970, 13–15
– "Looking for the beach under the pavement", RIBA-Journal, 1971, no. 8, 328–333
– "Huiswerk voor meer herbergzame vorm", Forum, 1973, no. 3, 12–13
– "Het gebouw als instrument voor de bewoner", Wonen TABK, 1973, no. 5, 22
– "De te hoog gegrepen doelstelling", Wonen TABK, 1974, no. 14, 7–9
– "(Presentation)", Building Ideas, 1976, no. 2, 2–14 (also in Forum XXIV-3)
– "Strukturalismus-Ideologie", Bauen + Wohnen, 1976, no. 1, 21–24
– "Architecture for People", A+U, 1977, no. 75, 124– 146
– "El deber para hoy: hacer formas más hospitalarias", Summarios, 1978, no. 18, 3–32
– "Shaping the Environment", B. Mikkelides, Architecture for People, London 1980, 38–40
– "Motivering van het minderheidsstandpunt", Wonen TABK, 1980, no. 4, 2–3
– "Ruimte maken, ruimte laten", Wonen tussen Utopie en werkelijkheid, Nijkerk 1980, 28–37
– "Architektur für Menschen", G.R. Blomeyer en B. Tietze, In Opposition zur Moderne, Brauschweig 1980, 142–148
– "Un insegnamento de San Pietro", Spazio e Società, 1980, no. 11, 76–83
– "The tradition behind the Heroic Period of modern architecture in the Netherlands", Spazio e Società, 1981, no. 13, 78–85 (see also: Intermediair, 08.08.1980),
– "Einladende Architektur", Stadt, 1982, no. 6, 40–43
– "Het twintigste-eeuwse mechanisme en de architectuur van Aldo van Eyck", Wonen TABK, 1982, no. 2, 10–19 (Also in Dutch and English in: Aldo van Eyck, Amsterdam 1982, 7–27)
– "De schetsboeken van Le Corbusier", Wonen TABK,

1982, no. 21, 24–27

– Collegedictaat (book for students) part A,
"Het Openbare Rijk", Oct. 1982

– "Montessori en ruimte", Montessori Mededelingen,
1983, no. 2, 16–21

– "Le Royaume Public" and "Montagnes dehors
montagnes dedans", Johan van der Keuken, Brussels
1983, 88–118

– "Una strada da vivere. Houses and streets make each
other", Spazio e Società, 1983, no. 23, 20–33

– "Un rue habitation à Amsterdam", L'Architecture
d'Aujourd'hui, 1983, no. 225, 56–63

– "Aldo van Eyck", Spazio e Società, 1983, no. 24, 80–97

– Collegedictaat (book for students) part B,
"Ruimte Maken – Ruimte Laten", March 1984

– "Building Order", Via, 1984, no. 7, 39–45

– "Over bouwkunde, als uitdrukking van denkbeelden",
De Gids, 1984, no. 8/9/10, 810–814

– "L'Espace de la Maison de Verre", L'Architecture
d'Aujourd'hui, 1984, no. 236, 86–90

– Biennale de Paris, Architecture, 1985, Luik/Brussel
1985, 30–35

– "Stadtverwandlungen", Materialien (a sort of reader),
Hochschule der Künste-Berlin, no. 2, 1985

– "(Lecture)", INDESEM 1985, Delft 1985, 46–57

– "Architectuur en constructieve vrijheid",
Architectuur/Bouwen, 1985, no. 9, 33–37

– "Espace Montessori", Techniques & Architecture,
1985/1986, no. 363, 79–83 (French translation of the
article "Montessori en Ruimte"),

– Arnulf Lüchinger, Herman Hertzberger, 1959–86, Bau-
ten und Projekte/Buildings and Projects/Bâtiments et
Projets, (all descriptions of the projects are written by
Herman Hertzberger), Den Haag, 1987

– "Schelp en kristal", F. Strauven, Het burgerweeshuis
van Aldo van Eyck, Amsterdam 1987, 3 (also
published in English in 1996)

– "(Lecture)", INDESEM 1987, Delft 1987, 186–201

– "Henri Labrouste, la réalisation de l'art",
Techniques & Architecture, 1987/88, no. 375, 33

– Collegedictaat (book for students) part C,
"Uitnodigende Vorm", April 1988

– "The space mechanism of the twentieth century or
formal order and daily life: front sides and back
sides", Modernity and Popular Culture
(Alvar Aalto symposium), Helsinki 1988, 37–46

– INDESEM 1988, contains a summary of
Hertzberger's lecture during the International Design
Seminar in Split (Yugoslavia), 1988

– "Das Schröder-Haus in Utrecht",
Archithese, 1988, no. 5, 76–78

– "Het St. Pietersplein in Rome. Het plein als bouw-
werk", Bouw, 1989, no. 12, 20–21

– Library of Tape-slide Talks "Herman Hertzberger –
Reciprocity of human life and habitat", PAV 19/8806,
(cassette-tape with slides of a lecture of HH in Lon-
den, June, 1988)

– "Inleiding", Jan Duiker, Rotterdam 1990, 6–7

– "Hoe modern is de Nederlanse architectuur?", Rotterdam 1990, 61–64

– INDESEM 1990, contains a summary of Hertzberger's
lecture during the International Design Seminar at the
Technical University Delft, 1990

– "The Public Realm", A+U, 1991, April, 12–44

– "Joop Hardy: anarchist", Mag het'n beetje scherper
alstublieft?, Delft 1991, 143–144

– Lessons for students in architecture (book) revised pu-
blication, English edition, of the 3 books for students
(collegedictaten), part A, (1982/1984) "Het Openbare
Rijk", part B (1984) "Ruimte maken – ruimte laten",
part C (1988) "Uitnodigende Vorm", Rotterdam,
1991; second edition 1993 (translated in: German,
Japanese, Italian, Portuguese, Dutch, Chinese)

– "Introductory Statement", [p. 9–12] and "Do architects have any idea of what they draw?",
[p. 13–20], The Berlage Cahiers 1 – Studio '90 '92,
Rotterdam, 1992

– "(Lecture)", Nara, and Triennale, Nara, 1992, (extra
issue of The Japan Architect) reproduction of a lecture
of Herman Hertzberger in Nara (Japan) concerning his
own projects, 1993, no. 8, 147–152

– "De Cineac, toen en nu. Een bioscoop met visie",
Skrien, 1994, no. 197, 58–61

– "Klaslokalen aan een centrale leerstraat", Ruimte op
school, Almere 1994, 16–17

– "Das Unerwartete überdacht", Herman Hertzberger,
Projekte/Projects/1990 1995, (catalogue of the travel-
ling exhibition "Das Unerwartete überdacht/Accom-
modating the Unexpected", that was first exhibited in
Munich, January 1995), Rotterdam 1995, 4–15

– "Designing as Research", The Berlage Cahiers 3 –
Studio '93–'94, The new private realm, Rotterdam,
1995, 8–10

– "De architectuur", Chassé Theater, (book in Dutch and
English, published for the opening of the Chassé
Theater in Breda), Rotterdam 1995, 16–31

– "Learning without Teaching", The Berlage Cahiers 4 –
Studio '94–'95", Reflexivity, Rotterdam, 1996, 6–8

– "P.S.: vulnerable nudity!", Wiel Arets, Strange Bodies/
Fremdkörper, Basel/Boston/Berlin 1996, 65–67

– "A culture of Space", Dialogue, architecture + design
+ culture, Taiwan, 1997, 14–15

Mitarbeiter / Collaborators

May 1997

Herman Hertzberger
Cor Kruter
Henk de Weijer
Willem van Winsen
Heleen Reedijk
Folkert Stropsma
Roos Eichhorn
Dickens van der Werff
Geert Mol
Patrick Fransen
Ariënne Matser
Takeo Ozawa
Laurens Cobben
Romano van Hooren
Aaron Sprecher
William van Ingen
Chris Arts
Anat Stern
Jeroen Bayens
Marijke Teijsse
Colette Sloots
Ruud van Eck
Pia Elia
Helen Min

Former office members who worked in the office over a longer period; in random order

Rob Nord, Robert Stoek, Hein de Haan, Stephanie Smith, Hylke Hoekstra, Winfried van Zeeland, Jan Koning, Aicha Rahali, Janet Hortulanus, Dorle Schneider, Rob Blom van Assendelft, Henk Uytenhout, Anne Margreet Six-van Krimpen, Jan Beckers, George Thie, Kaoru Suehiro, Guido van Overbeek, Noriko Okuda, Hans Schotman, Sil Mantel, Manfred Kausen, Susana Rusch, Boudewijn Delmee, Thomas Maurer, Caroline van Raamsdonk, Nicolas Dodd, Ellen Mensingh-van der Meiden, Andrew Dawes, Menno Ongering, Bas Bossers, Rugier Timmer, Christine Machynia, Jan Peters, Erwin de Maar, Rogier Weyand, Marieke van Vlijmen, Rob Bannink, Stefan de Bever, Frans Bosch Reitz, Akelei Hertzberger, Niek van Vugt, Gundula Cordes, Dennis Pieprz, Jan Peter Wingender, Loes Blokker, Jolanda van der Graaf, Helen Dahm, Laurens Jan ten Kate, Mathis Müller, Martin Fredriks, Roswitha Düsterhoft, Nynke Joustra, Madeleine Haag, Paul Boluyt, Ariane Widmer, Peter de Bruin, Nicolas Pham, Peter van Ravenswaay, Hjördis Sigurgisladottir, Pien Linssen, Brechje Pronk, Rafael Gomez-Moriana, Ad Schreuder, Robert Brinksma, Bill Lobb, Tadej Glazar, Fergus Purdie, Tom Bergevoet, Jan Rietvink, Tom Corsellis, Margaret Sobieski, Uri Cohen, Marion White, Dolf Floors, Rijk Rietveld, Jan Richard Kikkert, Wim Oxener, Joke Witkamp, Andrea Fenwick-Smith, Penelope Dean, Jasper Etten, Remco van Bergen, Julien Descombes, Jan van den Berg, Mirjam IJsseling, Stefan Johansson, Sonja Spruit

Bildnachweis / Illustration Credits

All illustrations are reproduced courtesy of the Herman Hertzberger archives, Amsterdam, except as follows:

Dimitris Antonakakis
back cover
Bitter / Kerrebijn
141 bottom
Hein de Bouter
41 bottom, 51 top/middle/bottom
Martin Charles / Architectural Photography
81 top, 83 top, 85 bottom
Jan Derwig / Architectuur Fotografie / BFN
85 top, 162/163
Willem Diepraam
45, 52, 57, 58, 64 bottom
Herman van Doorn / Lock Images /GKF
front cover, 137, 147 top, 149 top, 148 top, 150, 151, 164, 167, 169
Frits Dijkhof Fotografie / BF
79 top
Hendriksen - Valk
70
Gerhard Jaeger
72 bottom
Manfred Kausen
47
Johan van der Keuken
36, 43, 74, 75 top
Jan Richard Kikkert
179 top, 180/181 middle
Atelier Klaus Kinold / Architektur-Publikationen
61 top, 76, 111 bottom right
KLM luchtfotografie
53
Bruno Krupp
54 top, 55 bottom
J. Kurtz
64 top
Jannes Linders
93 bottom
Duccio Malagamba
166 bottom, 168 top

Rudolf Menk / Beton Verlag GmbH
44
Geert Mol
161 top and bottom
Oerlemans van Reeken Studio
70
Uwe Rau
88/89
Reger Studios / Bilder Konzepte und Visionen
185 top right
Anda van Riet
188 left
Kaoru Suehiro
182
Izak Salomons
42 left
Paul Steunebrink Fotografie
75 bottom
Machteld Stikvoort
124 top and middle, 126 bottom
Peter Strobel Photodesign
77
Henk Tukker
60
United Photos de Boer
113 top right
Jan Versnel
39 top and bottom left
Cor Viveen
146 top
Marieke van Vlijmen
140 bottom
Ger van der Vlugt
69 top, 78, 87, 93 top, 110, 112 top left and bottom, 111 middle right, 113 bottom, 132 top
S. Voeten
144, 149 bottom, 153
Jens Willebrand
176/177
Kim Zwarts
135

Große Architekten in der erfolgreichen Studiopaperback-Reihe:
The Work of the World's Great Architects:

Alvar Aalto
Karl Fleig
4. Auflage. 256 Seiten,
600 Abbildungen
ISBN 3-7643-5553-0
deutsch / französisch

Tadao Ando
Masao Furuyama
2. Auflage. 248 Seiten,
397 Abbildungen
ISBN 3-7643-5437-2
deutsch / englisch

Mario Botta
Emilio Pizzi
2. Auflage. 256 Seiten,
666 Abbildungen
ISBN 3-7643-5438-0
deutsch / französisch

Johann Bernhard
Fischer von Erlach
Hellmut Lorenz
176 Seiten, 172
Abbildungen
ISBN 3-7643-5575-1

Walter Gropius
Paolo Berdini
256 Seiten, 580
Abbildungen
ISBN 3-7643-5563-8

Herzog & de Meuron
Wilfried Wang
2. Auflage. 160 Seiten,
313 Abbildungen
ISBN 3-7643-5589-1
deutsch / englisch

Philip Johnson
Peter Blake
256 Seiten, 270
Abbildungen
ISBN 3-7643-5393-7
deutsch / englisch

Louis I. Kahn
Romaldo Giurgola,
Jaimini Mehta
4. Auflage. 216 Seiten,
423 Abbildungen
ISBN 3-7643-5556-5
deutsch / französisch

Le Corbusier
Willi Boesiger
7. Auflage 1994.
260 Seiten, 525
Abbildungen
ISBN 3-7643-5550-6
deutsch / französisch

Adolf Loos
Kurt Lustenberger
192 Seiten, 332
Abbildungen
Deutsche Ausgabe:
ISBN 3-7643-5586-7
Englische Ausgabe:
ISBN 3-7643-5587-5

Richard Meier
Silvio Cassarà
208 Seiten, 264
Abbildungen.
ISBN 3-7643-5350-3

Ludwig Mies van der
Rohe
Werner Blaser
6. erw. Auflage,
248 Seiten, 180
Abbildungen
ISBN 3-7643-5619-7
deutsch / englisch

Richard Neutra
Manfred Sack
2. überarbeite Auflage.
192 Seiten, 291
Abbildungen
ISBN 3-7643-5588-3
deutsch / englisch

Jean Nouvel
Olivier Boissière
300 Seiten, 300
Abbildungen
ISBN 3-7643-5356-2
deutsch / englisch

Andrea Palladio
Die vier Bücher zur
Architektur
A. Beyer und U. Schütte
4., überarbeitete Auflage.
472 Seiten
ISBN 3-7643-5561-1

Richard Rogers
Kenneth Powell
208 Seiten, 481
Abbildungen
ISBN 3-7643-5582-4
deutsch / englisch

Aldo Rossi
Gianni Braghieri
4., erweiterte Auflage.
288 Seiten, 290
Abbildungen
ISBN 3-7643-5560-3
deutsch / französisch

Hans Scharoun
Christoph J. Bürkle
176 Seiten, 182
Abbildungen
Deutsche Ausgabe:
ISBN 3-7643-5580-8
Englische Ausgabe:
ISBN 3-7643-5581-6

Karl Friedrich Schinkel
Gian Paolo Semino
232 Seiten, 330
Abbildungen
ISBN 3-7643-5584-0

Gottfried Semper
Martin Fröhlich
176 Seiten, 192
Abbildungen
ISBN 3-7643-5572-7

José Luis Sert
Jaume Freixa
2. Auflage. 240 Seiten,
500 Abbildungen
ISBN 3-7643-5558-1
deutsch / französisch

Alvaro Siza
Peter Testa
208 Seiten, 300
Abbildungen
ISBN 3-7643-5598-0
deutsch / englisch

Mart Stam
Simone Rümmele
160 Seiten, 167
Abbildungen
ISBN 3-7643-5573-5

Luigi Snozzi
Claude Lichtenstein
224 Seiten, 260
Abbildungen
ISBN 3-7643-5439-9
deutsch / englisch

Louis Henry Sullivan
Hans Frei
176 Seiten, 208
Abbildungen
ISBN 3-7643-5574-3
deutsch / englisch

Giuseppe Terragni
Bruno Zevi
208 Seiten, 490
Abbildungen
ISBN 3-7643-5566-2

Oswald Mathias Ungers
Martin Kieren
256 Seiten, 406
Abbildungen
ISBN 3-7643-5585-9
deutsch / englisch

Otto Wagner
Giancarlo Bernabei
2. Auflage. 208 Seiten,
330 Abbildungen
ISBN 3-7643-5565-4

Frank Lloyd Wright
Bruno Zevi
3. Auflage. 288 Seiten,
575 Abbildungen
ISBN 3-7643-5557-3
deutsch / französisch